DATE DUE

FEB 2 3			

Demco No. 62-0549

THE WORKING LIFE

A Samurai
Warrior

THE WORKING LIFE

A Samurai Warrior

TITLES IN THE WORKING LIFE SERIES INCLUDE:

An Actor on the Elizabethan Stage

The Cavalry During the Civil War

A Civil War Doctor

A Colonial Craftsman

A Medieval Knight

A Medieval Merchant

A Medieval Monk

A Mountain Man on the American Frontier

A Renaissance Painter

A Roman Gladiator

A Roman Senator

A Sweatshop During the Industrial Revolution

A Worker on the Transcontinental Railroad

THE WORKING LIFE

A Samurai Warrior

ADAM WOOG

LUCENT BOOKS

An imprint of Thomson Gale, a part of The Thomson Corporation

THOMSON
™
GALE

Detroit • New York • San Francisco • San Diego • New Haven, Conn.
Waterville, Maine • London • Munich

THOMSON
GALE

Acknowledgment
My thanks for research advice to Dr. Theodore C. Bestor, professor of anthropology and
Japanese studies at Harvard University—also known as my old college pal Ted.
—AW

LIBRARY OF CONGRESS CATALOGING-IN-PUBLICATION DATA

Woog, Adam, 1953–
   A samurai warrior / by Adam Woog.
     p. cm. — (The working life series)
Includes bibliographical references and index.
Summary: A portrayal of the work of a Samurai warrior, including how they trained for
war, their code of conduct, the weapons they used, and the independent Samurai
(ronin).
   ISBN 1-59018-583-8 (alk. paper)
   1. Samurai—History. I. Title. II. Series.
DS827.S3W66 2005
952'.02'088355—dc22
                                                      2004025781

Printed in the United States of America

CONTENTS

FOREWORD

"The strongest bond of human sympathy outside the family relations should be one uniting all working people of all nations and tongues and kindreds."
Abraham Lincoln, 1864

Work is a common activity in which almost all people engage. It is probably the most universal of human experiences. As Henry Ford, inventor of the Model T said, "There will never be a system invented which will do away with the necessity of work." For many people, work takes up most of their day. They spend more time with their coworkers than with family and friends. And the common goals people pursue on the job may be among the first thoughts that they have in the morning, and the last that they may have at night.

While the idea of work is universal, the way it is done and who performs it vary considerably throughout history. The story of work is inextricably tied to the history of technology, the history of culture, and the history of gender and race. When the typewriter was invented, for example, it was considered the exclusive domain of men who worked as secretaries. As women

workers became more accepted, the secretarial role was gradually filled by women. Finally, with the invention of the computer, the modern secretary spends little time actually typing correspondence. Files are delivered via computer, and more time is spent on other tasks than the manual typing of correspondence and business.

This is just one example of how work brings together technology, gender, and culture. Another example is the American plantation slave. The harvesting of cotton was initially so cumbersome and time consuming that even with slaves its profitability was doubtful. With the invention of the cotton gin, however, efficiency improved, and slavery became a viable agricultural tool. It also became a southern tradition and institution, enough that the South was willing to go to war to preserve it.

The books in Lucent's Working Life series strive to show the intermingling of work, and its reflection in culture, technology, race, and gender. Indeed, history viewed through the perspective of the average worker is both enlightening and fascinating. Take the history of the typewriter, mentioned above. Readers today have access to more technology than any of their historical counterparts, and, in fact, though they would find the typewriter's keyboard familiar, they would find using it a bore. Finding out that people spent their days sitting over that machine (with no talk of carpal tunnel syndrome!) and were valued if they made no typing errors because corrections were cumbersome to make and, in some legal professions, made documents invalid, is an interesting story that involves many different aspects of history.

The desire to work is almost innate. As German socialist Ferdinand Lassalle said in the 1850s, "Workingmen we all are so far as we have the desire to make ourselves useful to human society in any way whatever." Yet each historical period offers a million different stories of the history of each job and how it was performed. And that history is the history of human society.

Each book in the Working Life series strives to tell the tale of these anonymous workers. Primary source quotes offer veracity and immediacy to each volume, letting the workers themselves tell their stories. In addition, thorough bibliographies tell students where they can find out more information, and complete indexes allow for easy perusal of the text. While students learn about the work of years gone by, they gain empathy for those who toil and, perhaps, a universal pride in taking up the work that will someday be theirs.

THE RISE OF THE SAMURAI CLASS

The samurai of old Japan were larger than life: fierce warrior-knights, proud devotees of the martial arts, loyal disciples of a strict moral code. For hundreds of years, they were also Japan's single most powerful social force, imposing the will of their masters on the rest of the population. The samurai and their exploits continue to fascinate, although they have long since passed into legend.

LAND

The samurai held sway between roughly the ninth and the nineteenth centuries. The social structure of their world was, in many ways, similar to that of medieval Europe. A tiny number of aristocratic families controlled the country's wealth and power, dominating the lower classes of farmers, artisans, and merchants.

These noble families were headed by lords called daimyo. (The title lit-erally translates as "great name.") Their wealth came from vast land holdings that were passed down, generation to generation, within a family. Since Japan's economy was based on agriculture, control of the land was crucial. Historian Louis Fréderic notes, "To own land (with, of course, its peasantry, the manpower required for farming it) was as good as possessing wealth, and consequently, power."[1]

Usable land was precious. Because of its mountainous terrain, only about 20 percent of Japan's land was suitable for farming. Competition for control of it was fierce. Ruling families wanted to expand their prized territory and protect what they already had. A class of warriors, the samurai, arose to serve that need. (In fact, the word *samurai* stems from a word meaning "servant to nobility.")

SAMURAI AND DAIMYO

Over time, the samurai developed into a clearly defined social class of their own. Members of this class married only other samurai (or, occasionally, nobility). In this way, samurai traditions of service remained strong.

During this time, a well-defined relationship developed between the samurai and the daimyo. The daimyo promised to support their warriors with salaries, gifts, or income from the farming of parcels of land. In return, the samurai promised to protect and extend their lords' property, by force if necessary.

The bond was very close, with every samurai pledging absolute loyalty to his master. This close relationship is illustrated by a comment from one thirteenth-century samurai. He wrote to his son that duty to one's master and a good heart "are like two wheels of a carriage, and of these it is duty that is the making of a samurai."[2]

This loyalty was not one-sided, however. Each daimyo also took care to treat the samurai under him well. Historian H. Paul Varley writes, "In return for the loyalty and service he rendered his lord, the vassal [servant] expected both protection and reward."[3]

A COMPLEX SOCIAL SYSTEM

Although samurai were the servants of aristocrats, they enjoyed a high degree of prestige within Japanese society. This society was a complex structure that had evolved over centuries. It relied on a strict division between the social classes.

❧ A CLASS APART ☙

Strictly speaking, the term samurai referred to just one rank within the larger warrior class called bushi. *Hideyoshi Toyotomi, one of the three shoguns who unified Japan under military rule, moved decisively to separate the various social classes of Japan, establishing the samurai above all others except the imperial family. Writer Harry Cook, in his book* Samurai: The Story of a Warrior Tradition *notes:*

To minimise the chance that anyone might rise in rebellion against his rule, Hideyoshi wanted to disarm the peasants and on August 29, 1588 he ordered that all peasant-weapons should be surrendered.

Hideyoshi maintained that he wanted the weapons gathered together so they could be melted down to make nails and spikes, which would be used in the construction of a huge statue of the Buddha. This pious work would serve a number of purposes; as well as helping the people to gain merit in this life and the next, it would impede peasant uprisings against the government.

One important social effect was the clear distinction that would now have to be made between the samurai, who were allowed to carry weapons, and the peasants, who were not. The beginnings of the rigid social structures that developed . . . can be traced to this policy, and to the census Hideyoshi ordered to be carried out in 1590. This classified people according to their occupation, and made it difficult, if not impossible, to move from one class to another.

Seen here blowing his war trumpet, Hideyoshi Toyotomi helped unify Japan under a single ruler in the sixteenth century.

At the top of this structure was the emperor, who was considered divine. Below the emperor and his family were the nobility—the daimyo and their families—followed by the samurai class. Next in status were the peasants. Compared with other feudal societies, the status of Japanese peasants was relatively high. They werc held in esteem because they were responsible for food cultivation, and without them the nation would have starved. Below the peasants came the artisans who made goods for people to use or consume. Merchants who dealt in those goods were near the bottom, and at the lowest rung were "untouchables," who carried out unclean jobs such as tanning animal hides or cleaning toilets.

Each class was divided into many subgroups. For example, the samurai class ranged from wealthy, top-ranking warriors to low-level soldiers who barely had enough to eat. Each subgroup had a specific title, pay range, and degree of prestige.

Class membership was hereditary. If a boy's father was a samurai, he would also one day be a samurai. However, there were occasional exceptions. Japanese society had a complicated system of formal adoption that meant that in certain circumstances a nonsamurai could be adopted into a samurai family and gain full status as a samurai.

THE SHOGUNATE

The imperial family was the highest social class, but the emperor's political role was largely ceremonial. He had little real power, with no ability to collect taxes, enforce laws, or even declare war. The emperor and his imperial court lived in isolated splendor, barely connected to the outside world.

Real, if unofficial, power belonged to the daimyo—as many as 150 of them, each controlling his individual region. For many centuries, attempts to unify this scattered power failed; instead, there was chaos and frequent warfare. This situation slowly changed, however.

The change began in the late twelfth century when a daimyo named Yoritomo Minamoto became shogun, or supreme general. The shogun was the ceremonial leader of the emperor's military forces. This role traditionally was temporary and involved little real authority. Yoritomo managed to make it both permanent and powerful, marking the beginning of the military's dominance over Japanese government.

THREE LEADERS

Despite the newfound power of the shogun, Japan was not unified under a single leader until the late 1500s and early 1600s. During this period, three shoguns in succession were able to establish order.

The first of these, Nobunaga Oda, was notable for introducing brilliant military innovations, including the first large-scale use of firearms. He also established many laws that dramatically affected the samurai. For example, he formally separated the warrior class from the rest of society. In earlier times, samurai typically farmed in peacetime and soldiered only in wartime. Nobunaga made these mutually exclusive jobs. Scholar Stephen Turnbull remarks, "The achievement of Nobunaga . . . was to produce a professional corps of samurai who did nothing but fight, while the farmers did nothing but till the land."[4]

Nobunaga's successor, Hideyoshi Toyotomi, raised the status of the samurai nearly to that of the nobility. He also changed the way they lived and worked. For example, under his rule only samurai and daimyo had the right to wear and use swords; lower classes thus effectively had no access to serious weapons.

THE TOKUGAWA ERA BEGINS

Hideyoshi's successor, Ieyasu Tokugawa, built on the accomplishments of Nobunaga and Hideyoshi to finally unify the country. A popular saying is that Nobunaga piled the rice, Hideyoshi kneaded the dough, and Ieyasu ate the cake. In other words,

Ieyasu Tokugawa defeated rebel daimyo and established himself as the uncontested ruler of Japan in the early 1600s.

all three were needed to complete the job—and Ieyasu reaped the benefits.

Ieyasu, a canny politician and diplomat, lavishly rewarded his allies and ruthlessly punished his enemies. He was also a skilled military leader, whose two decisive victories against rebel daimyo, the Battle of Sekigahara in 1600 and the siege of Osaka Castle in 1615, effectively ended any opposition to his rule. So successful was Ieyasu that for more than 260 years an unbroken succession of Tokugawa-

Throughout the Tokugawa era, members of the samurai class like this warrior wielded tremendous political power.

related shoguns ruled. This span of time became known as the Tokugawa era.

The Tokugawa era was a period of unquestioned military dominance in Japan. The samurai comprised only about 7 to 10 percent of Japan's population. However, they enjoyed near-total power over Japan's political, economic, military, and social life. Paradoxically, the Tokugawa era was also a time of peace. This was because the shogunate used its military strength to enforce strict order. However, the nation lived in a state of armed peace, what Stephen Turnbull summarizes as "a peace that is more the absence of war."[5]

The power the samurai class enjoyed was only a reflection of each individual warrior's strength. This strength, in turn, was the result of rigorous, lifelong training.

CHAPTER 1

TRAINING FOR WAR

The samurai in pre-Tokugawa years were primarily professional warriors. They did other work, such as farming, but a samurai's main job was going to battle on behalf of his master. It was natural, therefore, that the samurai spent the bulk of their training in the study of conflict. Still, the samurai strove to balance hard, physical training with more refined and intellectual pursuits. As historian H. Paul Varley notes, "One of the most intriguing features of the samurai character was the merger of the aesthetic and the killer instincts."[6]

THE MARTIAL ARTS

Although purely intellectual or aesthetic topics were important parts of his education, the martial arts lay at the core of any samurai's training. These combat disciplines emphasized the importance of physical fitness, stamina, and fighting one on one.

Collectively, the martial arts were called *kyuba no michi*, the Way of Horse and Bow. Individually, there were dozens of specific styles.

Many of these techniques had existed for centuries even before the rise of the samurai. Some had been imported from China, Korea, and elsewhere in Asia. However, these martial arts reached an especially high point of development during the samurai era. Many experts argue that they have never been surpassed. Martial arts writers Oscar Ratti and Adele Westbrook assert, "The Japanese experience in, and contribution to, the theory and practice of individual combat, armed and unarmed, is certainly among the most ancient, sophisticated, and enduring ever recorded."[7]

A common goal of all the martial arts was to train the mind, spirit, and body to be instantly ready for combat.

Whether in a large-scale, protracted war or an individual duel, the samurai had to be prepared at all times. As one warrior put it, "The samurai must never relax his guard. Even when alone with just his wife, he should not forget to have his sword at hand."[8]

EARLY TRAINING

Training for this lifetime of readiness began at about age five. At that point, the sons of samurai were taught to ride horses. They were given their first practice weapons (such as wooden swords), and they began wearing child-sized versions of traditional samurai clothing, such as distinctive kimonos (wraps) and trousers. These clothes, as well as hairstyles and other clues, immediately identified the wearers as samurai.

Formal instruction in the martial arts began around age thirteen, though frequently sooner. Typically, fathers or other relatives were the chief instructors. Families that could afford it often paid for private instruction as well.

৶ STRICT REGULATIONS ৳

This passage, reprinted in Stephen Turnbull's Samurai Warriors, *is an excerpt from a document that details regulations for raising troops for an important daimyo family named Hojo.*

Sashimono must be black and new. [Sashimono were banners attached to the backs of soldiers on the battlefield.]

Helmet crests may be either gold or silver. [One assumes that lacquer, and not actual precious metal, is intended.]

The shaft of the pike [spear] must be covered in leather.

Children are not to be brought to camp.

Shields are to be two and a half feet long, one foot wide, and half an inch thick. [This must refer to the wooden shields planted in the ground as a protection for the arquebus (rifle) troops, though they sound unusually narrow.]

Armour is not to be rolled up. It is to be placed in an armour box. The haori [jacket] should also be cared for and ready for use.

Mounted warriors should ride a horse worth one-third of your grant. Although having a horse is troublesome, you must not starve it.

As for your equipment, take care so that it will not be damaged by the elements. The haori should be made of black cotton. Torn flags and rusty pikes are strictly forbidden.

The fortunate young men who received special training attended one of the many academies in Japan that specialized in one or another of the martial arts. Warrior monks or former samurai typically ran these schools. Each school had its own set of loyal former students who subscribed to the particular philosophies of their teachers.

Whatever he trained for, every samurai studied a basic curriculum that included three aspects of armed combat: swordsmanship, archery, and the use of the spear. Students were expected to become proficient in each of these types of combat. The famous samurai Musashi Miyamoto, in his book *Go Rin no Sho* (The Book of Five Rings), emphasized the importance of this proficiency when he wrote, "The way of the warrior is to master the virtue of his weapons."[9]

Kenjutsu, or sword fighting, was especially highly developed. To study it, students typically used *bokuto*, full-size wooden practice swords, before graduating to the use of real swords. Whether using practice swords or real ones, students of *kenjutsu* had to learn dozens of specific and complex techniques. For example, they needed to master the basic stances taken when preparing to fight. They also had to spend hours practicing repetitive actions such as drawing one's sword from its sheath and replacing it, until such actions became second nature.

Even seemingly simple actions, such as controlling one's breath or understanding the proper way of gripping the sword handle, had to be carefully studied.

There were also dozens of more advanced techniques to learn. For instance, students had to be able to size up an opponent immediately, judging the other's skill level and fighting style. Among other advanced techniques to be learned were such maneuvers as forcing an enemy to make the first move, avoiding the striking range of the enemy, fighting in a tightly enclosed space, and fighting against several enemies at once.

Studying *kenjutsu*, as with all the martial arts, was a hands-on practice. It was not uncommon for students to sustain significant stab wounds or gashes during practice sessions. "Learn by being cut" was a familiar motto.

THE BOW AND ARROW

Practice in using the bow and arrow, called *kyujutsu*, was also considered crucial to a warrior's training. This practice was often done on horseback. A typical exercise was to stand straight up in the stirrups of one's saddle and shoot arrows at small wooden targets as the horse galloped past. As with all the martial arts, this maneuver required fierce concentration. Students were not allowed to let their bodies sway away from their

A samurai warrior poses with his sword in this nineteenth-century photo. The samurai devoted much of their time to mastering the art of sword fighting.

proper positions. Even at the moment of releasing an arrow, and with fast horses beneath them, the samurai were expected to remain perfectly steady.

Bow and arrow practice was not always on horseback. It was also done on foot. Students practiced by firing volleys of arrows while running forward at top speed.

Students used a variety of targets. Sometimes they were fixed. For example, instructors might have their students shoot at silhouettes of deer, made of deerskin and marked to point out the animal's most vulnerable

This model outfitted in a suit of armor and armed with a bow gives some idea of the imposing appearance of the samurai.

spots. Other common fixed targets were round boards covered in hide and stuffed with straw or other material.

Other times, archery students went after moving targets—that is, live animals. Occasionally, dogs were used as targets. Usually, though, student samurai ventured into forested land, stalking such animals as deer and a fierce wild boar called *inoshishi*. Hunting was a way to put dinner on the table, but it was also excellent training, since it gave students the opportunity to handle real, full-sized weapons. It also gave them experience in outthinking a canny, unpredictable, moving target in an unfamiliar environment.

THE SPEAR

The third basic weapon in armed-combat training was the spear. Many elite samurai thought spears were lowly instruments, suitable only for foot soldiers—not top-level soldiers like themselves. Nonetheless, practice with the spear was part of any student warrior's basic regimen.

Like sword practice, spear training involved a practice weapon—in this case, a long pole with a padded tip. These practice spears were made entirely of wood, unlike real spears, which were tipped with iron or steel blades. Nonetheless, they were heavy enough to inflict painful injuries if students, practicing with each other or their masters, were careless or overzealous. Serious bruises and broken bones were not uncommon.

UNARMED COMBAT

Not all training for a future samurai involved weapons. Another important component of the martial arts was unarmed, hand-to-hand combat. Collectively, these unarmed techniques were called *bugei.* As with sword practice, there were many specialized variations.

One such variation was jujutsu (also called jujitsu). Jujutsu emphasized disabling an enemy by using the enemy's own weight and momentum to force him off balance. Like many forms of *bugei,* it relied heavily on intelligence and speed, not simply on brute strength.

Other specialized techniques of unarmed combat that a young samurai could learn included *hojutsu,* the art of binding an enemy with a short cord; *sueijutsu,* the art of swimming and treading water while in armor; *fukumijutsu,* which involved spitting needles in an enemy's eyes; and *saiminjutsu,* the art of hypnotizing an enemy.

❧ MANY STYLES OF MARTIAL ARTS ❧

In 1815, a set of eighteen major types of martial arts (there were many more minor styles) was identified by an anonymous samurai scholar. The list is reprinted in Stephen Turnbull's The Lone Samurai and the Martial Arts:

archery

horsemanship

dakyu [a game somewhat like mounted lacrosse, in which two teams of seven men tried to get balls into a net set in the middle of a field]

equestrian [mounted] archery

swimming a horse

swimming

straight spear

sickle and chain

curved spear

sword

grappling [jujutsu]

sword drawing

roping

baton

grappling in armor

throwing weapons

gunnery

firearms

MENTAL CONDITIONING AND STAMINA

Training in the martial arts was not only physical. Much of the work involved mental conditioning. This aspect of martial arts stressed the importance of training one's mind, spirit, and body to work as one unit. For instance, young samurai were made to practice shooting arrows, or swinging swords, over and over in exactly the same way. In time, such movements became so familiar that they could be performed without thinking. In real combat, things happened quickly and without warning; there was no time to think about technique. Writer Harry Cook notes, "When training with the sword—or with any other weapon— the warrior was taught to be aware of his surroundings and his opponent, so that he was always prepared for a surprise attack."[10]

Other exercises built stamina. These included fasting, sometimes for days at a time, going on long marches without rest, and maintaining rigid postures for long periods without complaining or showing distress. Young samurai also were frequently made to rise after only a little sleep, study for hours before breakfast, then walk long distances—perhaps barefoot in the snow—to the houses of their teachers. Alternatively, small groups of students might be forced to stay up all night together, reading their lessons aloud in turn.

Instilling courage in the face of death was typically another element of a young samurai's education. The idea was to accustom students to death so that they would not flinch when confronted with it later. Students were thus given such tasks as running errands that took them through cemeteries late at night. Japanese folklore was full of ghost stories, and a fear of ghosts was strong, so trips to the cemetery made for rigorous training.

Sometimes lessons in the realities of death were quite graphic. Samurai scholar Inazo Nitobe writes, "[N]ot only were small boys sent to witness [executions], but they were made to visit alone the place [of execution] in the darkness of night and there to leave a mark of their visit on the trunkless head."[11]

A BALANCED EDUCATION

Martial arts, physical stamina, and mental conditioning were not the only things that future samurai learned. They were also required to balance their combat training with the study of such intellectual disciplines as art, poetry, religion, and history.

These studies were considered just as important to a warrior's future working life as the more physical activities. In *Bushido Shoshinshu*, a book of advice for young warriors, the samurai Shigesuke Taira wrote, "While it goes without saying that an

Two samurai warriors engage in battle on a bridge. Samurai combat was physically taxing, and warriors trained hard to increase their stamina.

attitude of hardness and strength is considered foremost in the way of the warrior, if strength is all you have you will seem like a peasant turned samurai, and that will never do. You should acquire education as a matter of course, and it is desirable to learn things such as poetry . . . little by little, in your spare time." [12]

Beginning at about age seven, samurai boys began formal schooling in these gentler pursuits. If their families could afford it, boys attended elite temple schools and studied these subjects under Buddhist monks.

Humbler private schools were typically organized in each village for those who could not afford to attend temple schools.

THE FINER PURSUITS

Regardless of where boys studied, two important topics were military history and the strategy of warfare. A working knowledge of famous battles, for example, was considered essential. It was important to appreciate the ways in which armies could be victorious. It was also important to appreciate why an army was defeated in a

A samurai warrior in full armor prepares for battle. The samurai observed strict rules of etiquette when engaging the enemy in battle.

specific battle and how one could learn from those mistakes. Norikage Asakura, a famous samurai of the late fourteenth and early fifteenth centuries, once wrote, "A general of great merit should be said to be a man who has met with at least one great defeat."[13]

Other commonly taught topics were calligraphy (artistic penmanship), art, the tea ceremony, ethics, flower viewing and arranging, poetry, religion, and history. An appreciation of Buddhist sutras (prayers) and poems and the classics of Japanese and Chinese literature was considered especially important. The study of such subjects helped to focus a samurai's mind and served as a balance to his warlike pursuits.

The ability to compose original poetry was especially prized. Writing poems, it was thought, served to refresh a student's mind after more physically demanding exercises. Louis Fréderic writes, "Outdoor games alternated with extremely serious lessons in writing and literature. In his leisure moments [a student] would delight his mind by composing verses."[14]

Although young samurai differed in their mastery of all these topics, virtually every samurai could read and write; the literacy rate neared 100 percent. This was in stark contrast to the peasant class, the next rung down in society, of whom only about 20 percent were literate.

ETIQUETTE

Etiquette was another important part of training. Good manners were crucial in Japanese society, especially for the samurai. It was important for them to speak and act properly at all times. Nagauji Hojo, a samurai of the fifteenth and sixteenth centuries, noted, "One should always be genteel in his speaking. A man shows his inmost self by a single word."[15]

The system of social etiquette was highly developed, and there were countless rules that samurai in training had to learn. Some of these rules, for example, pertained to the proper handling of swords—such as the rule that a samurai could never touch another warrior's scabbard (sword sheath) with his own scabbard. To do so, even accidentally, was a deep insult and grounds for an immediate fight because it was a point of honor that a samurai could only touch or handle his own sword.

Other rules for proper sword etiquette concerned the use of swords inside a house. Students learned that when visiting a fellow samurai, for example, a warrior never kept his sword on. Instead, he surrendered it to a servant just inside the door; the servant handled it with a silk cloth (never with the bare hand) and placed it on a special rack. However, students learned, a samurai was allowed to keep his short sword, since he was expected never to be completely unarmed.

Still other aspects of etiquette training involved learning to wash, dress, and present oneself properly. Yuzan Daidoji, in his handbook *Code of the Samurai* (written in the early eighteenth century), spelled out some of these rules. All samurai, he wrote, "must wash their hands and feet night and morning and take a hot bath. . . . A samurai must do his hair every morning and keep the hair properly shaved from his forehead. Then he must always wear the ceremonial dress proper to the occasion and of course wear his two swords as well as carry a fan in his girdle."[16]

THE TEA CEREMONY AND HEAD REMOVALS

One aspect of etiquette was of paramount importance: *cha-no-yu*, the formal tea ceremony. This ancient ceremony was a slow, solemn ritual involving precise, stylized movements. Each object used in the ceremony carried symbolic meaning. For example, utensils were identified with the Five Elements, as identified by Chinese philosophy: Charcoal (the equivalent of the element Wood) was used to build a Fire, which boiled Water in an iron (Metal) kettle; this, in turn, was used to make tea in a ceramic bowl (Earth).

The tea ceremony had multiple purposes. It was a welcoming, sociable way to bind a host (who made the tea) and his guests (who drank it) together in an intimate way. It was also a form of profound meditation. On one level, therefore, studying the tea ceremony taught young samurai manners and gracefulness. But its strong spiritual and religious aspect also directed a samurai's thoughts away from the everyday world, helping him achieve a rigorous personal discipline.

Cha-no-yu thus was seen as a perfect melding of the aesthetic and the physical, a balance that young samurai strove to maintain. Writer Harry Cook notes, "The ideal samurai were expected to [be] capable of bringing the same finesse to the subtle complexities of the tea ceremony as they would to the removal of an enemy's head on the battlefield."[17]

BECOMING A FULL SAMURAI

Only after years of intensive training and instruction were boys considered ready to be samurai. At about the age of fifteen, each underwent a coming-of-age ceremony to mark this occasion. It was called a *genbuku*.

The *genbuku* ceremony included several important rituals. One involved adopting the distinctive samurai hairstyle. The top of the head was shaved, and the remaining hair, kept long, was oiled and gathered in a tight bun. According to some sources, the shaved top of the head symbolized maturity, although it may also

❧ CORRECT THOUGHTS ❧

Shingen Takeda was a warrior, high-ranking samurai, and lay Buddhist monk of the sixteenth century. A follower recorded Shingen's comments, some of which are reprinted in Harry Cook's Samurai: The Story of a Warrior Tradition:

Learning is to a man as the leaves and branches are to a tree, and it can be said he should not be without it. Learning is not only reading books, however, but is rather something that we study to integrate with our own way of life. One who was born into the house of a warrior regardless of his rank or class, first acquaints himself with a man of military feats and achievements in loyalty, and in listening to just one of his dictums each day, will in a month know 30 precepts. Needless to say, if in a year he learns 300 precepts, at the end of that time he will be much the better.

Thus, a man can divide his mind into three parts: he should throw out those thoughts that are evil, take up those ideas that are good, and become intimate with his own wisdom. . . . I would honour and call wise the man who penetrates this principle, though he lacks the knowledge of a single Chinese character. As for those who are learned in other matters, I would avoid them regardless of how deep their knowledge might be.

have served simply to make helmet-wearing more comfortable.

During the *genbuku* ceremony, the new samurai's godfather gave him a special new name. The honoree also received new clothing. These items included a fine silk kimono, a special style of trousers called *hakama*, and a ceremonial headdress called an *eboshi*, which was a stiff cap of black silk. Finally, the new samurai was presented with the greatest gifts of all: two swords, one short and one long. From then on, he had the right, responsibility, and honor to wear these swords whenever he went out.

Technically, a samurai was allowed to take part in battle once he had gone through the *genbuku* ceremony. However, many samurai were in their early twenties before they saw serious conflict, primarily because older and more experienced samurai were available to fill the daimyo's fighting ranks.

Formal instruction in the martial arts and other aspects of a samurai's training continued long after the *genbuku* ceremony. Although formal instruction typically ended at about the age of twenty-two, in practice most samurai never fully stopped. Maintaining one's skills was a lifelong occupation.

A young man in samurai dress (right) poses with his mother and sister. Although women could be members of the samurai class, they were still expected to be subservient to the men.

Ieyasu, the founder of the Tokugawa shogunate, was a good example of this lifelong commitment. He swam regularly in the moats of Edo Castle, his main fortress, into his seventies. He was also a good shot with the bow and arrow, practicing daily nearly until his death at age seventy-three. And all his life he remained a passionate devotee of the tea ceremony.

TRAINING FOR WOMEN

The development of physical and mental capabilities was almost completely reserved for men. As in Japanese society as a whole, women were not on an equal footing with men, even though samurai women were considered part of the same social class. Still, although they were expected to be subservient, they were also expected to be strong and brave. They were therefore typically taught to defend themselves.

This usually meant instruction in using the dagger and the *naginata*, the spear most often used by foot soldiers. Such knowledge was important if a woman's husband was at war or away on official business, since during wartime women and old men were often the only ones left to defend a village or castle; able samurai males (the only ones who could be armed) would be a rarity; most were fighting or already dead. Furthermore, women were expected to kill themselves rather than face the dishonor of capture, so they needed to know how to use the dagger on themselves.

Samurai women also received detailed instruction (usually from their mothers) in more mundane matters, such as running households. Although a samurai wife was not the absolute authority in her house, she held an important position. For example, she typically controlled the household budget and managed the servants.

A woman's relationship with her husband resembled that of a samurai with his lord; it was built on absolute loyalty. A wife was expected to center her life on her home and family. At meals, for instance, she served everyone else in the family before partaking of the food herself.

Perhaps a samurai woman's most important job was to educate the youngest children and the girls in her house. She had the task of instilling in them the ideals and principles of their class. These included unquestioning obedience to one's lord and a knowledge of religious and moral principles. Such principles were called Bushido—the Way of the Warrior.

CHAPTER 2

BUSHIDO: THE WAY OF THE WARRIOR

The clans of fierce warriors from which the samurai originally developed were rough and uneducated and followed no special rules of conduct. These early samurai had virtually only one rule: to take what they could for themselves and their lords. According to scholar Mitsuo Kure, this made the early samurai little more than a collection of gangsters: "They were a kind of 'mafiosi,' who fought for family, land and plunder, but scarcely for honor."[18]

However, the attitude and philosophy of the samurai changed dramatically in later centuries. This was because they began to rise in prominence and power, eventually becoming an elite class in their own right. As their role shifted, the samurai gradually developed a strict and complex code of conduct.

BUSHIDO

These rules of conduct were called Bushido, or the Way of the Warrior.

They were aimed at balancing a warrior's rough side with smoother, more refined manners and morals. Yuzan Daidoji, in his book *Code of the Samurai*, wrote, "Though Bushido naturally implies first of all the qualities of strength and forcefulness, to have this one side only developed is to be nothing but a rustic samurai of no great account."[19]

The code of Bushido governed the ways in which a samurai should think, act, and be at all times. It outlined specific moral values a samurai should hold. It thus controlled nearly all facets of a samurai's working life.

Young samurai—boys and girls both—began learning the complex rules and ideals of Bushido at an early age. Study of Bushido, and reflection on its meanings, continued all through one's life. This study was absolutely essential; the sixteenth-century samurai

Bokuden Tsukuhara, considered one of the greatest swordsmen in Japanese history, commented, "A samurai who does not know the way of the warrior is like a cat that does not know the way of ratting."[20]

THE THREE ESSENTIALS

The Way of the Warrior had many variations, and there was never a single, obligatory set of Bushido laws that every samurai followed. In fact, for centuries Bushido was passed down only as an oral tradition; it was not codified into more or less final form until the Tokugawa era.

Bushido thus differed slightly depending on one's location, generation, and teacher. Different teachers taught different versions, emphasizing what they felt was most important. According to scholar Inazo Nitobe, "It [Bushido] was founded not on the creation of one brain, however able, or on the life of a single personage, however renowned. It was an organic growth of decades and centuries of military career."[21]

Nonetheless, certain basic themes and characteristics remained constant and became part of the lives of all samurai. These basic elements centered on an absolute sense of devotion, obligation, and bravery. As the samurai Shigesuke Taira wrote in his book *Bushido Shoshinshu*, "On the warrior's path, only three things are considered essential: loyalty, duty, and valor."[22]

LOYALTY

As a whole, Bushido stressed the importance of positive personal characteristics. Among the most prominent of these were loyalty to one's master, willing self-sacrifice, ethically correct behavior, and self-discipline. Also important was a refined sense of justice, of shame, and of honor. Refined manners, as well as purity and modesty in

---

❧ THE SEVEN ❧ ESSENTIAL PRINCIPLES

All samurai followed as closely as possible the basic principles of Bushido, the Way of the Warrior. This complex set of moral codes varied considerably over time and place, but it was traditionally summarized in seven words:

Gi: rectitude, making the right decision, including the correct time to die

Yu: heroic bravery

Jin: compassion

Rei: right action and courtesy to others

Makoto: sincerity and truthfulness

Meryo: honor and glory

Chugo: devotion and loyalty.

Pictured is a seventeenth-century painting of Confucius, the Chinese philosopher on whose teachings the samurai code of Bushido is based.

one's thoughts, were crucial. And frugality, mercy toward others, and affection toward fellow samurai were also highly prized values.

Much of Bushido was rooted in the concept of virtue espoused by Confucius, a Chinese philosopher whose ideas migrated to Japan in the third century A.D. Confucius taught that good things flow naturally if a person leads a life of virtue—that is, of ethical behavior, self-sacrifice, respect for one's elders, and self-discipline. He wrote, "Let but a prince cultivate virtue, people will flock to him; with people will come to him lands; lands will bring forth for him wealth; wealth will give him the benefit of right uses. Virtue is the root, and wealth an outcome."[23]

Loyalty was another Confucian concept that became a cornerstone of Bushido. A samurai was honor-bound to be loyal to his daimyo—even to the point of dying in his defense. Harry Cook notes, "The obligations incurred when a samurai entered a lord's service demanded that, in return for the lord's protection, he should willingly sacrifice everything, including his life, to protect his lord's interest."[24] Although dying honorably in the service of one's master was crucial, Bushido also taught that dying foolishly was no virtue. Rather, choosing the proper moment for one's death was important. According to one anonymous samurai, "To rush into the thick of battle and to be slain in it is easy enough, but it is true courage to live when it is right to live, and to die only when it is right to die."[25]

THE RELIGIOUS ROOTS OF BUSHIDO

Such precepts were strongly influenced not only by Confucianism, but also by Japan's other dominant religions. These other religions were Shintoism and Buddhism. Each contributed elements that fit in well with the tough, disciplined life of a samurai. (Some samurai followed Christianity after the introduction of that religion to Japan in the sixteenth century. By then the con-

cepts of Bushido were firmly established, however, so Christianity had little impact on samurai philosophy.)

Shintoism was the earliest spiritual belief to take root in Japan. It had a strong element of worship of the natural world. According to Shinto beliefs, many gods controlled various aspects of the world. One of these was Hachiman, the fierce war god.

The Shinto god Hachiman, shown here in the guise of a monk, was a fierce war god that held special significance for the samurai.

Hachiman held a special status and significance for the samurai, who regularly prayed at temples dedicated to him.

Like the other religious roots of Bushido, Buddhism fit in well with the working life of a samurai. This faith had arisen in India in the sixth century B.C., spread quickly across Asia, and was introduced to Japan by missionaries from China and Korea in the sixth century A.D.

Several Buddhist sects and offshoots developed in Japan and became extremely popular. One of these variants, Zen Buddhism, exerted a powerful influence on Bushido. Zen stressed the importance of living a simple life of denial, discipline, and self-control. It also taught that no one should fear death. Zen further emphasized the need for a detachment from the everyday world. It stressed that change is inevitable, that the world is impermanent, and that human life is temporary. According to Zen, suffering derives from an attachment to material things, and an enlightened mind can achieve tranquillity and fearlessness by forsaking such attachment.

The fact that three separate religions provided the ethical underpinnings for Bushido meant that the Way of the Warrior was sometimes at odds with one religion or another. For instance, a samurai was expected—even compelled—to kill other men and animals. This put him in conflict with Buddhist teachings, which stressed a reverence for living things. Historian Louis Fréderic writes, however, that such seeming paradoxes did not trouble the samurai, who focused not on the contradictions but on the congruence of Bushido and religious beliefs:

[A samurai] worshipped in the first place the ancestral gods of his clan or his family and the kami [Shinto gods] who protected both himself and his fellow men; in this respect he was Shintoist. The samurai also observed the moral principles of obedience, loyalty and filial piety [respect for elders] which were derived from the Confucian system of ethics. He worshipped the Buddhist divinities, he believed in universal impermanence, in retribution of good and evil in a future life, and in a paradisian [paradise-like] life after death and, in this, he could claim to be a Buddhist.[26]

ACCEPTING DEATH

Despite the teaching that dying foolishly was no virtue, one of the primary attributes of Bushido was its emphasis on fearlessness in the face of death. The samurai were famous for being willing, even happily so, to die in the service of their lords. Tsunetomo

A samurai warrior holds a dying comrade in this nineteenth-century painting. The code of Bushido taught samurai to fight without fear of dying.

Yamamoto, a famous samurai of the late seventeenth and early eighteenth century, expressed this aspect of Bushido simply: "The way of the warrior, I've found, is to die."[27]

The acceptance of death as a natural outcome of a samurai's work formed a central tenet of Bushido.

Accepting death willingly was a simple matter of honor. And upholding honor—one's own or that of one's daimyo—was paramount. According to Naoshige Nabeshima, a samurai of the late fifteenth and early sixteenth centuries, "No matter whether a person belongs to the upper or lower ranks,

❧ ON DYING ❧

The proper attitude toward death was a crucial part of Bushido. The writer-samurai Yuzan Daidoji, in this passage from his book Code of the Samurai, *reflects on the subject:*

The samurai . . . has to set before all other things the consideration of how to meet his inevitable end. However clever or capable he may have been, if he is upset and wanting in composure and so makes a poor showing when he comes to face it all, his previous good deeds will be like water and all decent people will despise him so that he will be covered with shame.

For when a samurai goes out to battle and does valiant and splendid exploits and makes a great name, it is only because he made up his mind to die. And if unfortunately he gets the worst of it and he and his head have to part company, when his opponent asks for his name he must declare it at once loudly and clearly and yield up his head with a smile on his lips and without the slightest sign of fear. . . .

In times of peace the steadfast samurai, particularly if he is old but no less if he is young and stricken with some serious disease, ought to show firmness and resolution and attach no importance to leaving this life. Naturally if he is in high office . . . while he can speak he should request the presence of his official superior and inform him that as he has for long enjoyed his consideration and favor, he has consequently wished fervently to do all in his power to carry out his duties. . . .

This done, he should say farewell to his family and friends and explain to them that it is not the business of a samurai to die of illness after being the recipient of the great favors of his lord for so many years, but unfortunately in his case it is unavoidable. But they who are young must carry on his loyal intentions and firmly resolve to do their duty to their lord, ever increasing this loyalty so as to serve with all the vigor they possess. . . . Such is the leavetaking of a true samurai.

if he has not put his life on the line at least once he has cause for shame."[28]

Honor was intimately connected with death, especially in a battle situation. Yuzan Daidoji wrote in the early eighteenth century, "For the man who would be a warrior, regardless of high or low rank, his very first consideration should be the quality of his physical end, when his fate runs out."[29] To the samurai, surrender was not an acceptable option. Death freed the spirit and was thus infinitely preferable to the indignities of being taken prisoner. Fighting to the death, or committing suicide, were therefore the only honorable choices on the battlefield. A samurai warrior facing inevitable defeat refused to submit to the enemy. Instead, he found a secluded place and committed suicide.

Breaking even a single tenet of the Way of the Warrior was to risk bringing dishonor on oneself, and dishonor often was punishable with death, so samurai also committed suicide in a variety of circumstances other than losing a battle. Stealing, plotting treachery, or any number of lesser offenses carried the death penalty, although a samurai was generally given the option of taking his own life rather than outright execution. If he died in this honorable way, he avoided dishonoring his family and his daimyo no matter what offense he committed.

SEPPUKU

The form of suicide the samurai developed was a highly stylized ritual called seppuku. Seppuku allowed them to commit suicide (on the battlefield or elsewhere) with a maximum amount of dignity. This dignity was of paramount importance, as Shigesuke Taira noted in his book for young samurai, *Bushido Shoshinshu:* "The foremost concern of a warrior, no matter what his rank, is how he will behave at the moment of his death."[30]

Seppuku involved self-disembowelment—that is, cutting open one's own belly so that the intestines spilled out. (The ritual was sometimes called hara-kiri. However, this term, which literally means "to cut the belly," was considered vulgar and was never used by samurai.)

Seppuku was performed in a highly stylized and well-defined way. The man who was about to kill himself first knelt down. (On the battlefield, warriors carried a special deer hide to be used for this purpose.) He then loosened his clothing and cut himself deeply in the belly—across and up—using a short dagger. Despite the excruciating pain, it was considered poor form to show any distress. The samurai was expected to maintain a close hold on his emotions, even in the process of dying.

On the battlefield, this painful form of suicide, in which a warrior took a long time to die, was often the only option. However, if another samurai was available to help, a quicker (but no less honorable) style of seppuku was possible. This was typically the case if a samurai was captured and condemned to death.

If a second man was available he acted as a backup whose job was to ensure quick death. This second, or *kaishakunin*, to the condemned man was always a samurai. The second stood behind the condemned man and cut off his head as soon as the abdomen cuts were made, thus avoiding prolonged pain. (In battle situations, an enemy samurai sometimes acted as a samurai's *kaishakunin*.)

The *kaishakunin* had to be an experienced swordsman, capable of cleanly slicing the condemned man's neck—but not completely cutting his head off. The ideal situation was to leave the head slightly attached to the neck. In this way, someone chancing upon the body later would not mistake an honorable incident of seppuku for the execution of a common criminal, whose head would have been completely severed.

During the Tokugawa era, the role of the *kaishakunin* grew in importance. He evolved from one who prevented excessive pain to one who was the actual executioner. To avoid the pain of slicing one's belly open, it became acceptable to have the *kaishakunin* cut off the condemned man's head just as he reached for the knife. Sometimes the doomed man did not use a knife at all; he reached instead for a ceremonial, symbolic fan.

BUSHIDO IN DAILY LIFE

The principles of Bushido did not cover only weighty matters such as virtue and death. They extended also to how a samurai should conduct himself in many of the mundane matters of everyday life. For example, proper rules of etiquette and the maintenance of aristocratic manners were important elements of the warrior's code. Shigesuke Taira, writing in the early seventeenth century, noted some of these:

The principles of knighthood include washing your hands and feet and bathing morning and night, keeping your body clean, shaving and dressing your hair every morning, dressing formally according to the season and circumstances, and always keeping your fan in your belt, not to mention your long and short swords. When dealing with guests, you treat them courteously according to their status, and avoid useless talk. Even when you partake of a bowl of rice or a cup of tea, you are always careful not be slovenly.

If you are in public service, when off duty you do not simply lounge around; you read, practice

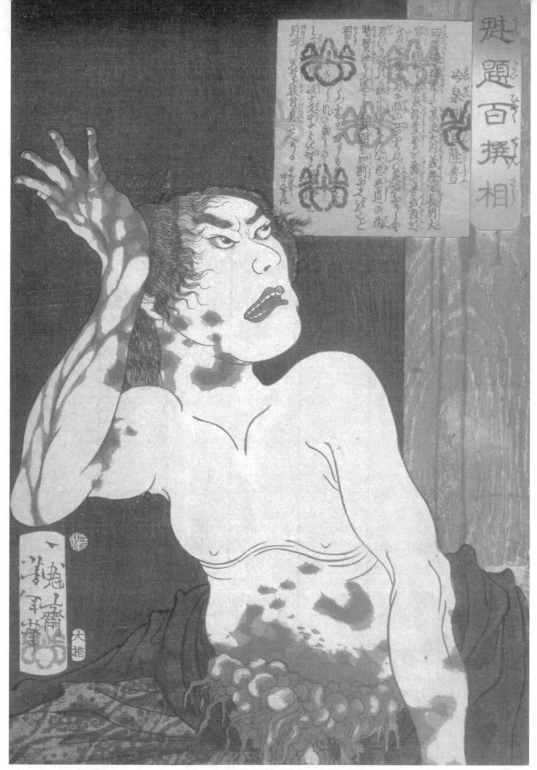

A samurai warrior commits suicide through self-disembowelment. A samurai warrior defeated in battle often killed himself in this way in order to die with honor.

☙ WITNESSING SEPPUKU ❧

In 1868, Lord Redesdale, then a British diplomat, observed a ceremonial suicide. A samurai had been ordered to commit seppuku for attacking foreign settlements in Hyogo (now Kobe). Harry Cook quotes Redesdale's memoirs in Samurai: The Story of a Warrior Tradition:

Slowly, and with great dignity, the condemned man mounted on to the raised floor, prostrated himself [bowed] twice, and seated himself. . . .

One of the three attendant officers then came forward, bearing a stand . . . on which lay the wakisashi, the short sword or dirk of the Japanese. This he handed . . . to the condemned man, who received it reverently, raising it to his head with both hands, and placed it in front of himself. . . .

[The condemned man] allowed his upper garments to slip down to his girdle and remained naked to the waist. Carefully, according to custom, he tucked his sleeves under his knees to prevent himself from falling backwards, for a noble Japanese gentleman should die falling forwards. Deliberately, with a steady hand, he took the dirk that lay before him; he looked at it wistfully, almost affectionately; for a moment he seemed to collect his thoughts for the last time, and then, stabbing himself deeply below the waist on the left-hand side, he drew the dirk slowly across to the right side, and, turning it in the wound, gave a slight cut upwards.

During this . . . he never moved a muscle of his face. When he drew out the dirk, he leaned forward and stretched out his neck; an expression of pain for the first time crossed his face, but he uttered no sound.

At that moment, the kaishaku [second] sprang to his feet and poised his sword for a second in the air; there was a flash, a heavy, ugly thud, a crashing fall; with one blow the head had been severed from the condemned man's body.

A silence followed, broken only by the hideous noise of the blood throbbing out of the inert heap before us, which but a moment before had been a brave and chivalrous man.

calligraphy, contemplate ancient stories or ancient warrior codes. Whether you are walking, standing still, sitting down, or reclining, in your conduct and manner you carry yourself in a way that exemplifies a genuine warrior.[31]

LIVING UP TO THE IDEAL

The samurai were expected to be paragons of virtue and strength, combining superior battle skills with the high moral and ethical concepts of Bushido. However, to live by all of the virtues laid out in Bushido was a superhuman ideal—and the samurai were merely human. Not all of them could, or would, comply with all of the principles of Bushido. In real life, even if one wanted to, living a completely virtuous life was not always easy or even possible. Historian Louis Fréderic writes,

These fine sentiments [of Bushido], professed by so many samurai . . . as well as by the women of their households, were not however universal, and history records a good number of examples of cowardliness, treachery, perfidy and useless cruelty. . . . Harsh men, inured to suffering, resigned to the blows of fortune, the samurai of the Middle Ages were none the less men with all the human frailties that this condition implies.[32]

This moral failing was especially apparent during periods of intense warfare. Lofty ethical concepts such as fair play and mercy could easily be forgotten or ignored in the heat of battle. Furthermore, Buddhist notions such as compassion for other living things were not always observed by the samurai. Despite the Bushido ideals of mercy and compassion, samurai could be ruthless in dispatching their rivals and were known to kill commoners for doing nothing more serious than neglecting to bow deeply.

Because the samurai could not live up to their unattainable ideal, they were guilty of many isolated but not uncommon acts of cowardice, deceit, treachery, thieving, and other acts of unworthy of a follower of Bushido. There are, for instance, many recorded instances of betrayal, on the battlefield or in the equally treacherous world of daimyo courts. Samurai were even known to switch allegiance on the battlefield, moving from a losing side to a victorious one. Historian H. Paul Varley writes, "There are many examples of samurai who remained true in the face of all adversity. At the same time there are more than sufficient cases of outright treachery and transference of allegiance from one side to the other, even in the midst of battle, to disabuse us of any notion that samurai warfare was all gallantry and high conduct."[33]

GOOD MEN AND BAD MEN

Such instances of less-than-perfect behavior were most common during the period of chaotic warfare in the fifteenth and sixteenth centuries, before military rule unified Japan. All too often, fathers murdered sons or sons murdered fathers in pursuit of their own gain. Ruthless outlaw clan leaders became powerful figures quickly, and treaties were broken without regard for justice. Writer Clive Sinclaire notes, "Although there were individual

A group of samurai beheads an enemy. The finer points of the Bushido code were often neglected in the heat of battle.

acts of bravery and examples of well-organized clans, these were in a distinct minority."[34]

On the other hand, the samurai were frequently capable of acts of mercy, such as sparing the lives of vanquished foes they had every right to kill. This was especially true after the Tokugawa shogunate imposed

military rule and the laws of the land began to be strictly enforced. Louis Fréderic notes, "If the epic tales [told about samurai] sometimes reveal what seems to be savage cruelty, cruelty which was dictated to them more by what they believed to be their duty as a warrior than by nature, they also describe them in moments when, freed from their social responsibility, they are filled with tenderness, even towards their enemies."[35]

Sometimes, good men who ordinarily did their best to uphold the ideals of Bushido could be led astray. A wise samurai was one who recognized that bad companions can easily corrupt such a man. Sadayo Imagawa, a samurai of the late thirteenth and early fourteenth centuries, noted, "Just as water will conform to the shape of the vessel that contains it, so will a man follow the good and evil of his companions."[36]

These companions, more often than not, were men of the same rank. Within the world of the samurai, these ranks were carefully defined and separated. Each had its own job description and typical set of weapons.

SAMURAI RANKS AND WEAPONS

As was true throughout all of feudal Japan, the warriors serving under a daimyo were strictly divided according to rank and class, with many subrankings within these. At the top were high-level generals and elite mounted warriors. Of lesser rank were archers, armor bearers, and *ashigaru*, or foot soldiers. At the bottom were laborers such as porters and animal attendants, who were generally still of the samurai rank.

Typically, a man entered service in the same rank his father had held. If he proved himself worthy, the samurai might rise to a higher rank. Usually, however, men were promoted only within whichever of the two main divisions they originally entered. In other words, it was unusual for a low-ranking samurai to rise to elite status.

However, there were a number of exceptions. One notable case was Ieyasu, the founder of the Tokugawa dynasty. Ieyasu began life as the son of a lower-ranking samurai and rose to prominence through his personal merits and cunning.

THE RANKS

The exact number of soldiers serving a particular family, and their specific rankings, differed according to the individual daimyo. However, there were certain commonly used groupings. A typical structure might feature ten ranks of samurai, five ranks in the upper echelon and five in the lower.

In the upper echelon, the highest-ranking soldiers were called *karo*. These were almost always mature, experienced warriors. *Karo* served as generals on the battlefield during times of war. In peacetime, they acted as advisers to the daimyo or as the heads of major departments within the daimyo's administration.

Among the low-ranking soldiers, most numerous were the humble *ashigaru* (foot soldiers). *Ashigaru* were frequently looked down on by other samurai. Not until the introduction to Japan of firearms in the sixteenth century did these lowly soldiers gain in status. Since elite mounted warriors scorned rifles as unsporting, the lowest ranks were initially trained to use them. Then, historian Louis Fréderic writes, as the new weapons proved their usefulness in battle, "these infantrymen proved to be increasingly necessary and eventually became indispensable."[37]

♨ RULES ♨

This passage is an excerpt from Buke-sho Hatto, *"Rules for Governing Samurai Houses," first published in 1615. The document, drawn up by the shogun Ieyasu's administration, governed behavior for daimyo families and their high-ranking samurai. It is reprinted in Stephen Turnbull's* The Book of the Samurai: The Warrior Class of Japan.

These rules subtly and indirectly allowed the shogunate a strong measure of control. For instance, the restriction on new buildings was a device to invite the daimyo and their samurai to contribute money, labor, and materials toward more castles for the shogun.

The study of literature and the martial arts must be practiced at all times.

Drunkenness and lewd behavior must be avoided.

Lawbreakers must not be hidden in any domain.

Daimyo must expel any samurai charged with treason or murder.

Residence in a fief [plot of feudally owned land] is to be restricted to men born in that fief.

The shogun authorities must be informed of any intended repairs to castles. Any new construction is forbidden.

Any plots or factions discovered in a neighboring fief must be immediately reported.

Marriages must not be privately contracted.

Visits by daimyo to the capital are to be in accordance with regulations.

All costumes and decorations are to be appropriate to the wearer's rank.

Commoners are not to ride in palanquins [porter-carried conveyances].

Samurai are to live a frugal and simple life.

Daimyo must choose men of ability to advise them.

PAY

As might be expected, a samurai's rank determined his pay. Salaries were traditionally measured in *koku*, the amount of rice required to feed one man for one year (about five bushels). In the early centuries of the samurai era, the salary was sometimes literally paid in rice and sometimes in equivalent amounts of other goods, money, or income-producing land. Over time, this method was phased out in favor of cash salaries. However, the payments were still meted out using the traditional *koku* as a unit of measure.

The highest-ranking samurai received salaries high enough to sustain them and their families in luxury. For example, one daimyo's bylaws stipulated that his *karo* be rewarded with lands producing anywhere between fifteen hundred and ten thousand *koku*, depending on individual service. Even at the low end of the scale, this was sumptuous compensation. Lower ranks received commensurately smaller rewards. In this same daimyo's domain, for example, the four ranks beneath the *karo* received from fifty to fifteen hundred *koku*, depending on rank. This system continued downward to the lowest *ashigaru*, who received stipends of three to seven *koku* apiece—barely enough to maintain their families on a subsistence level.

Elite mounted warriors were highly ranked samurai who received very handsome salaries.

WEAPONS

As with pay, a samurai's weapons were determined

by his rank. Each rank was authorized to carry and use certain weapons. Naturally, the higher ranks were allowed better and more prestigious weapons. But even the lowliest horse grooms and baggage carriers were usually armed with swords and spears.

No matter the rank, it was always a point of pride to have one's weapons at the ready and in good order. Yuzan Daidoji, the writer-samurai, made this point when he wrote about weapons, "If they have to be improvised in a hurry it will be an obvious sign of carelessness and will provoke contempt."[38]

BOWS AND ARROWS

In the earliest centuries of the samurai era, the bow and arrow was the primary weapon for high-ranking warriors. It was, indeed, an essential part of an elite samurai's gear. Stephen Turnbull writes, "At this time the samurai was a mounted archer, whose bow was kept as ready as the Western gunfighter's six-shooter."[39]

The bow and arrow had certain clear attractions for these early samurai. Firing an arrow was a suitably elegant and graceful way to engage a foe. Also, an arrow could be fired from a safe distance, eliminating (or at least delaying) the need for hand-to-hand combat. Samurai expert Mitsuo Kure writes that this was highly desirable: "Even a samurai wanted to kill his enemy while they were still as far apart as possible, using the bow or at least the lance."[40]

Bows came in a variety of sizes and styles, but those designed for warfare were generally seven to eight feet long. They were made (generally by skilled craftsmen) of strips of bamboo, glued together in many layers (or tied with rattan) and bent at the ends. Bowstrings were made of hemp or animal sinew. Since bowstrings were prone to breaking, a warrior always carried extras into battle.

Quivers to hold arrows while riding into battle were worn on the right side, so that the arrows could be easily withdrawn and fired while riding. (All samurai—in fact, all Japanese people— were taught to make the right hand their dominant hand. Those who were naturally left-handed were forced to switch when they were children.)

Arrowheads were made in a variety of styles. One type had barbed tips that stuck into an enemy's flesh. Another made a whistling sound as it flew. This arrow could not do much damage, but it served two purposes. It was a loud signal to announce the start of a battle. It was also thought to be audible to the gods, alerting them that brave deeds were about to be performed.

DIFFERENT KINDS OF POWER

Compared to the firearms that came into use in later years, the bow and arrow was not an especially potent weapon. The effective range of a

A samurai warrior challenges two men to draw his bowstring. In early samurai history, the bow and arrow was the primary weapon for high-ranking warriors.

samurai-style bow was limited. Furthermore, an arrow shot from such a bow did not usually hit hard enough to kill a warrior, unless it happened to hit a point in the body not protected by armor.

Certainly, though, the bowmen had a certain mystique. For example, according to legend, a famous samurai named Minamoto no Tametomo once sank a warship with a single arrow, and his bow was supposedly so powerful that it took five men to pull the string back. In at least one case, a bowman's reputation worked to his disadvantage. According to a military history of 1156, this samurai was so fearsome that when his enemies captured him they dislocated his arms with a chisel to keep him from ever using a bow again.

As such stories suggest, the bow and arrow's lack of practical physical power was made up by its spiritual force. The samurai believed that their weapons had a strong spiritual quality, so the warriors were often superstitious about them. For example, the night guards at the emperor's court customarily plucked the strings of their bows as they made their rounds in the belief that the sound would keep evil spirits away.

"THE SWORD IS THE SOUL OF THE SAMURAI"

The bow and arrow began to decline in popularity in the late thirteenth century. Even as it became less important as an offensive weapon, however, the weapon retained its symbolic importance. For example, the samurai continued to use the ancient term *yumitori* (bowman) as an honorary title for any accomplished soldier.

The reason for the bow and arrow's decline in importance was a dramatic advance in the technology for making swords. Early Japanese swords had not been especially effective, since they were clumsy and their blades were easily dulled or broken. Such swords were used only as defensive weapons of the last resort.

However, in the late thirteenth century, Japanese sword makers began to perfect their art. They devised a complex manufacturing process, hardening the sword's steel by repeatedly heating the metal with fire, then folding it on itself before cooling it with water. The finished weapon's edge remained sharp and the steel remained elastic and flexible, bending under impact instead of shattering.

With these technological improvements, the sword was quickly adopted by samurai as the weapon of choice. Writing in the early eighteenth century, Yuzan Daidoji noted, "In ancient times, all samurai, high and low, considered archery and horsemanship as the first of the military arts, but more recently they prefer to practice with the sword and spear and then to value skill in riding."[41]

The sword eventually achieved such prominence that it became the primary symbol of the warrior class. One mark of this prestige was the Tokugawa shogunate's edict that only samurai could own or carry these treasured weapons. As Ieyasu himself put it, "The sword is the soul of the samurai."[42]

KINDS OF SWORDS

The classic samurai sword, called a *katana*, was indeed a formidable weapon. It was typically two to three feet long, not counting the handle. It was thin, single-edged, and curved, with an elaborately decorated grip.

The *katana* was lightweight, making it easier to draw and use than were the older, heavier styles of swords. Because it was lightweight, it was also more useful when a warrior was on foot. It was worn with the sharp edge up if a samurai was on foot and needed to be able to draw the sword and slash upwards at a mounted or standing foe in a single movement. Alternatively, it was worn with the sharp edge down if the samurai was on horseback and expected to be slashing downward at enemies who were on foot.

A relatively rare variation of this classic sword was the *nodachi* or long sword. This gigantic sword was clumsy but deadly. At six feet or more in length, it was longer than an average man was tall, and it was so heavy that a samurai did not carry it by himself into battle. Instead, a servant carried the sword, then held the scabbard while the samurai removed the weapon and wielded it.

By the late sixteenth century, the custom was for a samurai to carry two swords. In addition to his *katana*, a samurai also carried a daggerlike sword, between twelve and twenty-four inches long, called a *wakizashi*, which was typically used for close-in work. Samurai wore both swords at all times in public—and always on the left side, since all samurai were right-handed.

SPIRITUAL WORKS OF ART

The best swords were highly individualized and expensive works of art. They were lovingly crafted and beautifully decorated, with elaborate handles and scabbards. To own such a weapon was a great and rare honor. The samurai believed that their swords had mystical powers and contained noble fighting spirits. Clive Sinclair writes that this feeling was "in keeping with the ancient Japanese religion of Shinto which attributed a spiritual property to everything—animals, trees, rocks and mountains."[43] The warriors often gave their swords individual names.

The code of Bushido, however, cautioned the samurai against excessive emphasis on swords. A set of laws written for a daimyo's troops in about 1480 stated this warning in practical terms. It said, "Do not excessively covet swords and daggers made by fa-

As technological advances in the art of sword making were made in the thirteenth century, the sword gradually replaced the bow and arrow as the quintessential symbol of the samurai.

mous masters. Even if you own a sword or dagger worth 10,000 pieces, it can be overcome by 100 spears each worth 100 pieces. Therefore, use the 10,000 pieces to obtain 100 spears, and arm 100 men with them. Thus you can defend yourself in war."[44]

OTHER WEAPONS

In addition to bows and swords, the samurai sometimes used other weapons. The most common was a type of spear or lance called a *naginata*—a curved blade on a stick several feet long, sometimes counterbal-

anced with a heavy iron butt. Similar to the *naginata*, but with a straight blade, was the *yari*. These weapons were thrust or swung offensively, and defensively their wooden shafts were useful when parrying the thrust of an enemy's weapon.

However, spears were not as aesthetically pleasing as swords. Most high-ranking samurai held them in contempt, and they were primarily used by *ashigaru* and other samurai of low rank. In addition, women were trained to use them for defensive purposes.

⚜ PRECIOUS ⚜ SWORDS

In *Samurai: The Story of a Warrior Tradition*, Harry Cook relates a story about how keenly the samurai valued their swords above all other weapons—indeed, all other possessions. It involves Mitsuhide Akechi, a sixteenth-century samurai leader who was besieged in his castle by a rival, Hidemasa Hori. Facing certain death, Mitsuhide's primary concern was that his swords should survive.

He therefore sent a message to Hidemasa: "I have many excellent swords, which I have cherished all of my life . . . they are part of the heritage of Japan itself. I will die happy, if you will stop your attack for a short while, so that I can have the swords sent out." Cook notes, "Hidemasa agreed and the weapons were lowered from the castle walls, carefully wrapped in padding to protect them."

Another weapon typically used by low-ranking samurai was the *kumade.* This device, usually made from bamboo and iron, looked like a long, wide version of today's garden rake. Foot soldiers typically used *kumade* to bring down mounted soldiers by snagging their clothing or armor.

Various other minor weapons were also at the samurai's disposal. Among these were the *otsuchi*, a huge war mallet similar to a sledge hammer; a giant wooden club called a *tetsubo;* and the *ono*, a large war ax mounted on a six-foot-long pole. Mounted samurai did not use shields, but foot soldiers and bowmen sometimes protected themselves with portable wooden shields, about eight feet high, which they rested on the ground and pushed in front of themselves as they advanced or awaited the enemy's charge.

Sometimes a lethal weapon was not called for. For example, if a *yojimbo*, a samurai who moonlighted as a private bodyguard, captured a thief, he might want to keep him alive for questioning. In such a case, the *yojimbo* might simply injure the thief with a *bo*, a long staff made of oak. Stephen Turnbull writes,

> Yojimbo always kept a bo . . . beside their beds. . . . They would take the bo if they heard a door being forced, and tackle an intruder using the techniques of bojutsu rather than swordfighting. In . . . contrast to the popular image from the movies, to cut a man down in cold blood was not usually acceptable, so the oak bo was one way in which he could be restrained. It was in fact a very strong weapon.[45]

GUNS

Eventually, just as swords rendered bows and arrows obsolete, potent new weapons—guns introduced to Japan by Portuguese soldiers in the mid-sixteenth century—began to overtake swords. These crude firearms were called flintlocks, because the firing mechanism used a flint to create a spark that ignited the gunpowder charge.

These weapons were slow to gain popularity at first. They were cumbersome, prone to misfire, and difficult to reload. Furthermore, flintlocks could not be used in the rain, because wet powder did not burn.

Early on, elite samurai disdained guns, finding them unsporting and aesthetically unpleasing. However, as they saw how effective guns could

Armed with a straight-blade spear, a samurai warrior (left) prepares to do battle with another warrior armed with an enormous mallet (right).

be under the right conditions, the elite samurai accepted them. The driving force behind this change was Nobunaga Oda's aggressive push to unify the country. He was the first to use guns on a large scale; once Nobunaga's army proved their effectiveness, most daimyo began adding them to their own arsenals.

Guns were never considered essential, however; they represented simply one more type of weaponry at the samurai's disposal. Ironically, because the elite samurai disdained them, it was the lowliest samurai, the foot soldiers, who were most fre-

quently trained in the use of guns. Moreover, until much later, bowmen were still considered superior to gunners, both in prestige and practicality. (This was, in part, because a bowman could reload and shoot faster than a gunner could.)

As guns became more widely used, craftsmen all over Japan copied and improved the original Portuguese designs. However, since Japan was isolated from the rest of the world during the Tokugawa era, the technology did not greatly advance. The *ashigaru* of the mid-1800s used essentially the same type of firearm that their an-

Dressed in traditional and European military clothing, a group of Japanese warriors is armed with rifles. During the sixteenth century, firearms gained acceptance among the samurai.

❧ MORE POTS ❧ AND PANS THAN SWORDS

The demand for finely made swords declined in the seventeenth century and onward, as the samurai's role as an active soldier declined. Japanese swordsmiths turned their attention to mass-producing swords of inferior quality, most of which were exported to China and other countries. The plummeting demand for swords was so acute that in 1720 the swordsmiths in Kanazawa, a city on the Japan Sea coast, spent more time making pots and pans than swords.

cestors had used hundreds of years earlier.

HORSES AND ARMOR

Even as weaponry advanced, one of the most potent symbols of the elite samurai remained his horse. This was so even though the vast majority of samurai went into battle on foot; only the highest ranks of samurai were ever allowed to ride horses. In part, this was a question of prestige. Horses were expensive to buy and maintain, so it simply made financial sense to reserve for the elite minority the right to ride into battle.

Riding a horse into battle, then, was a great honor. It was, however, an honor that carried with it a distinct fighting advantage. A man on horseback, armed with a sword, was a far more effective fighter than a foot soldier armed with a spear. Horses were thus essential to any samurai army, despite the cost, and the grooms who looked after them were likewise crucial. The animals typically used were bred from hardy stock that had originated in Central Asia; they were short and sturdy, not especially speedy but with great stamina.

Mounted soldiers always went into battle wearing elaborate armor. (Unlike the battle horses used by medieval knights in Europe, Japanese combat horses were not protected by armor. However, their bits, saddles, and stirrups were elaborately styled and decorated.)

These mounted samurai wore lamellar armor, a style common throughout Asia at the time. Many small pieces of leather or lacquered metal, called lamellae, were laced together with brightly colored silk cords. Together, these lamellae formed a solid but flexible shield for the shoulders and body.

Lamellar armor had several advantages. Although it was flexible, it was effective at deflecting or absorbing blows from swords or arrows. It was also light; a typical suit weighed only about twenty-five pounds. And

A samurai warrior rides his horse into battle. Only the most elite samurai fought on horseback.

Japan, lamellar armor was frequently augmented with a solid metal breastplate that defended against bullets more effectively.)

PUTTING ON ARMOR

Samurai did not usually wear their armor except when actually in battle. At other times, they dressed in light cotton robes and trousers. When a samurai did put on his armor, he followed a solemn and time-consuming ritual.

First, he donned a loincloth or one-piece undergarment, a special kimono, and baggy pantaloons. He also wore a padded cap or scarf to keep his hair snug under his helmet. Then, in addition to the armor itself (body wrap, shoulder protectors, and other separate pieces), the warrior also put on leg protectors of padded cloth or leather and, over his arms, heavy cloth sleeves reinforced with leather or metal. His feet were typically shod only in simple sandals or boots made of leather or bearskin.

Finally, the warrior put on his helmet. This was typically made of iron and decorated with a crest that showed his rank and which daimyo he was affiliated with. (Some helmets had holes on the top through which a warrior could push his hair.) The front of his helmet often had a ferocious-looking iron mask called a *mempo*. A *mempo* protected the samurai's face, but it had disadvantages: It was hot and uncomfortable, cut down on

it was compact; an entire suit fit into a small box for storage or transport. Furthermore, because it was constructed in small sections, it was easily repaired if part was damaged. (After firearms came into use in

As samurai warriors put on the individual pieces of their armor, they observed a solemn and very time-consuming ritual.

A samurai's helmet was typically decorated to show his rank and affiliation.

visibility, and made it difficult to hear or give shouted orders. As a result, many samurai chose not to wear them.

All of this gear was for the mounted samurai. Foot soldiers had much simpler versions of this armor. The main part of a foot soldier's protective gear was the *domaru*, a tunic of lamellae that wrapped around his body. He also wore a peaked hat, usu-ally made of lacquered wood or leather, called a *jingasa*.

Whether he was mounted or on foot, an elite warrior or a common soldier, a samurai was usually just one cog in the machine—part of a complex and highly organized social order. However, not every samurai chose to be, or could be, part of this system. A small but im-portant number of samurai were mas-terless. These men were called ronin.

CHAPTER 4

THE RONIN

For the typical samurai, attachment to a daimyo—being part of the tight-knit group of an army unit—was crucial to his work and life. Most samurai believed that without a master to whom they could be fiercely devoted, they had no purpose. However, some samurai had no such attachment. These masterless samurai were called ronin.

WAVE MEN

The name for these soldiers derived from a force of nature: The word ronin literally translates as "wave man." To the Japanese, this term was appropriate, since it was thought that a masterless warrior was tossed about in life with no more direction than an ocean's wave. The classic ronin was a loner who traveled from town to town, armed only with his swords and his wits. Rootless and independent, the ronin found work whenever and however possible. Far from being a rogue or rascal, the classic ronin had a strict personal code of ethics that made him duty-bound to challenge evil and right wrongs. This classic image is summarized by historian Stephen Turnbull: "He is ruthless, a superior swordsman, and the victim of enormous wrong, which his never-ending and bloody journey seeks eventually to put right."[46]

WHY SAMURAI BECAME RONIN

A samurai might become masterless for any of a number of reasons. Some soldiers deliberately chose to become ronin. Typically, these warriors were wealthy enough, or independent-minded enough, to afford the luxury of becoming their own men. They opted out of the rigid social system of samurai life, taking on instead the life of a freelancer who worked when and for whom he pleased.

A ronin, or masterless, warrior learns martial arts.

Sometimes, a samurai requested temporary ronin status from his master in order to go on a particular mission. For instance, he might want to avenge the death of a friend. Taking temporary ronin status freed the samurai from obligation to his daimyo. As a masterless man, moreover, any action he took would be his own responsibility and therefore would not stain the reputation of his master.

However, the vast majority of ronin did not choose or request their free status. They became masterless samu-

rai because they lost the normal, assured station of the soldier's life. This could happen for any number of reasons. Perhaps a samurai's lord was defeated in battle and killed. Or perhaps the daimyo was deeply disgraced in some way, such as by scandal. In either case, the shogun typically confiscated the daimyo's castle and possessions and dispersed his troops, who then would become ronin.

In some cases, a ronin had simply been fired—that is, dismissed from the service of his master. Again, this could happen for any number of reasons. For example, the ronin might have broken some law or brought shame to his master's name through some other action. In some cases, it was a permanent dismissal; at other times, the ronin could return to his position if he reformed, redeemed himself, or paid his debt.

SHAME

Becoming a ronin was, of course, typically a disastrous turn of events for a proud samurai, since he no longer had the protection and status of his master—not to mention the regular income that his service provided. The sense of shame a ronin felt was particularly strong because of the high premium Japanese society placed on being part of a cohesive group. Faced with such disgrace, many samurai grew despondent and committed suicide rather than accept life as ronin.

Those who chose to accept life as ronin were subject to abuse, scorn, and contempt. Even peasants and merchants, who were relatively low on the social scale, often considered ronin untrustworthy and disreputable. Regular samurai were especially disdainful of masterless soldiers, since being a ronin went against all the norms of servitude expected of warriors. Ronin were thus frequently targets of humiliation, insult, or worse. In some regions of Japan, masterless samurai were held in such disregard that regular samurai could kill them without fear of official sanction for their actions.

REBEL FIGHTERS

Despite the shame of being a masterless samurai, during the chaotic period preceding the Tokugawa shogunate the numbers of ronin across Japan steadily increased. Their ranks reached a peak—an estimated 400,000—during the Tokugawa era. This increase was caused by several factors.

A major reason was that the Tokugawa government forced all of Japan's daimyo to drastically cut the size of their personal armies. This move was designed to keep the daimyo in check. The shogun wanted to make sure that the regional daimyo could never amass enough resources, including manpower, to mount a serious rebellion.

However, in a way the plan backfired. The increase in the number of ronin worked against the authorities. Many ronin had no sympathy for the government and its rigid laws, and after they became free they were happy to lend their support to rebellious daimyo.

Furthermore, because they were ronin already, these armed vagabonds could potentially band together and mount (or participate in) uprisings of their own. One such uprising was the Shimabara rebellion. This conflict, waged for three months in 1637–1638 on the southern island of Kyushu, pitted a group of ronin and rebellious peasants against the shogunate's army of fifty thousand. The ronin were fighting on behalf of the peasants, who were being tortured, burdened with crushing taxes, and otherwise persecuted by the Tokugawa regime (in part because they had accepted Christianity, which the Tokugawa shogunate adamantly opposed).

YOJIMBO

Some samurai, including many of those who fought at Shimabara, wandered far from home to fight. However, most did not in fact journey far from their hometowns, because they did not need to: There was usually plenty of work near at hand. This was especially true during the pre-Tokugawa period of chaos, when local warlords had frequent need for skilled freelance fighters.

❧ A DUEL ❧

In this passage, Sakujiro Yokoyama, a famous judo master who lived during the time of the samurai, recalls a duel between a ronin and three samurai. Yokoyama was quoted in E. J. Harrison's book The Fighting Spirit of Japan, *and the story is reprinted in "Sakujiro Yokoyama's Account of a Samurai Sword Duel," http://home. att.net/~hofhine/Samurai.html.*

The parties to the duel were a ronin and three samurai, as I have already said. The ronin was rather shabbily dressed, and was evidently very poor. The sheath of his long sword was covered with cracks where the lacquer had been worn away through long use. He was a man of middle age. The three samurai were all stalwart men, and appeared to be under the influence of sake [rice wine]. They were the challengers. At first the ronin apologized, but the samurai insisted on a duel, and the ronin eventually accepted the challenge. By this time a large crowd had gathered, among which were many samurai, none of whom, however, ventured to interfere.

In accordance with custom, the combatants exchanged names and swords were unsheathed, the three samurai on one side facing their solitary opponent, with whom the sympathies of the on-lookers evidently lay. The keen blades of the duelists glittered in the sun. The ronin, seemingly as calm as though engaged merely in a friendly fencing bout, advanced steadily with the point of his weapon directed against the samurai in the centre of the trio, and apparently indifferent to an attack on either flank. The samurai in the middle gave ground inch by inch and the ronin as surely stepped forward. Then the right-hand samurai, who thought he saw an opening, rushed to the attack, but the ronin, who had clearly anticipated this move, parried and with lightning rapidity cut his enemy down with a mortal blow. The left-hand samurai came on in his turn, but was treated in similar fashion, a single stroke felling him to the ground bathed in blood. All this took almost less time than it takes to tell. The samurai in the centre, seeing the fate of his comrades, thought better of his first intention and took to his heels. The victorious ronin wiped his blood-stained sword in the coolest manner imaginable and returned it to its sheath. His feat was loudly applauded by the other samurai who had witnessed it. The ronin then repaired to the neighbouring magistrate's office to report the occurrence, as the law required.

Even in times of relative peace, a ronin could usually settle in one town and make a decent living. Some became martial arts teachers. Others might forsake their samurai status, take religious vows, and enter Buddhist monasteries. Perhaps the most common job for a ronin, however, was as a *yojimbo*, a bodyguard.

Yojimbo were in demand, in large part, because bandits and thieves were commonplace throughout feudal Japan. Many different kinds of people thus found uses for *yojimbo* on a regular basis. Gamblers frequently hired them to protect their dens from robbers. Wealthy merchants traveling with valuable goods likewise hired *yojimbo* to accompany them on journeys or as protection against robbers at their warehouses or homes.

"CRAZED PEOPLE" AND CROOKED RONIN

Anonymous bandits and thieves were not the only dangerous people that *yojimbo* could keep away by using their fighting skills, bravery, and brains. Since official protection was almost nonexistent in small rural villages, the residents of these villages lived in constant fear of criminal gangs. Groups of townspeople, known as *machi-yakko* (servants of the town), often pooled their resources to hire *yojimbo,* who would help them fight these gangs. A *yojimbo* had a variety of methods available to protect a village. For example, he might train the villagers to be an effective fighting force, even if they were armed only with farming tools. Or he might set up a showdown so that he himself could pick off gang members one by one.

The roving gangs were called *kabukimono*—literally, "crazed people." *Kabukimono* were very distinctive,

adopting strange hairstyles and dress and using vulgar, specialized slang. Ironically, many *kabukimono*—if not most—were themselves former ronin who had turned to crime. This is perhaps no surprise. The fighting skills learned as a samurai could easily be applied to make money through robbery or extortion.

Among the typical schemes *kabuki-mono* gangs committed were protection rackets: The gang promised to "protect" a shop owner's place of business from being wrecked or burned—by the gang itself—in exchange for money. Another typical scheme was for a gang member to haunt a dojo (martial arts studio), hoping to challenge others. Since he was usually a talented swordfighter, the gang member generally won—and took a measure of cash, food, or sake (rice wine) as his prize.

KENGO

Although many ronin stayed close to home to earn their livings (legally or not), some really did live the life of the classic wandering warrior. These men were called *kengo*, master swordsmen. They chose to carry on a tradition, long held in Japanese religious and martial arts societies, of a warrior making long, solo pilgrimages in order to perfect his knowledge of the martial arts. The *kengo* would seek opponents in distant regions, then challenge them to duels. By doing this, the

In this nineteenth-century illustration, a group of yojimbo *protects a noblewoman as she leaves her palace.*

kengo believed, he could obtain personal spiritual enlightenment through hard work, perseverance, and the forgoing of personal comforts.

Noble motives were behind most journeys by *kengo.* A few swordsmen, however, were simply after whatever money they could find. Stephen Turnbull notes, "Whereas it was common for expert swordsmen . . . to travel the country seeking to have their skills tested and improved, others did it for personal gain, bringing disgrace upon what was originally a noble and chivalrous concept."[47]

These spiritual pilgrimages did not necessarily entail hardship, whatever the original intent might have been. One of the most renowned *kengo* was Bokuden Tsukahara, who was born in 1490 and whom many experts feel was the greatest swordsman in all of Japanese history. According to legend, Bokuden was not exactly a loner; on one of his journeys, eighty followers attended him. The life of a *kengo* apparently brought him riches as well; in addition to his followers, on this same trip Bokuden had three spare horses and three large hunting hawks, each one a lavish expense.

DEFEAT WITHOUT A SWORD

Kengo could also, on occasion, gain fame with their wits instead of their swords. Another story about Bokuden concerns the time he encountered a boastful samurai on a ferryboat. After terrifying other passengers with his bragging, the samurai challenged Bokuden, who had until then remained silent, to a fight. Bokuden politely refused, and the samurai loudly called the swordsman a coward and demanded to know the name of his school of martial arts.

Bokuden replied that he belonged to the Munekatsu-ryu, or "the style that wins without a sword." This seemingly flippant reply made the samurai angrier, and he ordered the boatman to stop at a nearby island. He wanted to teach the audacious Bokuden a lesson.

The boastful samurai leaped out as the boat came close to the beach, waving his sword and shouting at Bokuden to get off the boat too. Instead, Bokuden used the ferryman's pole to push the boat away from shore. The samurai was suddenly stranded, and as the boat left Bokuden called out to him that this was what he had meant by defeating someone without a sword.

MUSASHI

Perhaps the most famous example of the classic *kengo* as a wandering seeker of enlightenment was Musashi Miyamoto. Probably born in 1584, Musashi was feared and disliked by many, and he was by all accounts an unappealing fellow. He was disfigured by extremely bad eczema (a skin disease) and had a strong dislike of baths and clean clothes. Nonetheless, Musashi's brilliance as a swordsman earned him lasting fame.

Musashi took part in his first major duel at the age of thirteen. This was a *taryu jiai*, a duel between two

♫ TWO KINDS OF EYES ♬

As a writer, the renowned ronin Musashi Miyamoto is best known for Go Rin no Sho (The Book of Five Rings), *but he produced many other works, including* The 35 Articles on the Art of Swordsmanship. *In this passage, reprinted in Harry Cook's* Samurai: The Story of a Warrior Tradition, *Musashi reflects on observing one's enemy—and being observed—in a duel:*

Since olden days many opinions have been expressed about which part of an opponent one should look at [during a duel] but the majority of people have supported staring at an opponent's face. When so doing, the eyes should be narrower than usual, but the mind should be broad.

The eyeballs should not move and when the opponent is near they should be focused as though they were looking into the distance. In this way, a man can look at not only his opponent's face but at his whole body, thus being able to anticipate any offensive thrusts he might make. In my opinion, there are two kinds of eyes: one kind simply looks at things and the other sees through things to perceive their inner nature. The former should not be tense [so as to observe as much as possible]; the latter should be strong [so as to discern the workings of the opponent's mind clearly]. Sometimes a man can read another's mind with his eyes. In fencing it is all right to allow your own eyes to express your will but never let them reveal your mind.

An attendant holds up a mirror for the master kengo warrior, Musashi Miyamoto, whose tremendous swordsmanship earned him fame throughout Japan.

people from differing schools of swordsmanship held to demonstrate the superiority of one style over another. Musashi responded to a general challenge issued by Kibei Arima, a

---

❧ ESSENTIAL ❧ MATTERS

Musashi Miyamoto was the most famous ronin in Japan. In his book Go Rin no Sho (The Book of Five Rings), *Musashi collected his thoughts on Bushido, warfare, and other matters. This list of essential things that all samurai should study and practice is reprinted in Hiroaki Sato's* Legends of the Samurai:

Think of things that aren't evil.

Train yourself in the way [of swordsmanship].

Try your hand in various arts.

Know how things are done in various professions.

Be able to measure the gains and losses of everything.

Learn to be able to pass judgment on various professional matters.

Perceive and understand what you can't see.

Pay attention to the smallest detail.

Do nothing useless.

---

swordsman of the Shinto school. Using only a *bo*, the long wooden staff, Musashi blocked Arima's sword and knocked the older, more experienced man to the ground.

In 1605, when Musashi was about nineteen, he began his long journeys. He wandered from town to town, challenging any swordsmen he could find in an effort to improve his skills. Over the next eight years, Musashi fought at least sixty documented duels.

In separate battles in Kyoto, for instance, Musashi defeated two brothers of the Yoshioka family. Using a *bokuto*, a wooden practice sword, Musashi knocked the elder of the two brothers unconscious and broke his arm. The younger brother then challenged Musashi using his *nodachi*, the enormous battlefield sword, but Musashi killed him with just a regular sword. Disgraced, the first brother issued another challenge. He then secretly plotted to have his own followers attack Musashi together. However, Musashi heard of the plot and was prepared to take on the extra attackers. They were nonplussed by Musashi's composure, their careful plan went to pieces, and Musashi killed them one by one.

A LIFE OF DUELING

Musashi's most famous duel took place in 1612. Musashi challenged Ganryu Sasaki, the most famous swordsman of northern Kyushu, the southernmost of Japan's four main islands. They agreed to meet on a tiny island called Funajima.

The two made quite a contrast: Ganryu was handsome and popular, while the unknown Musashi was his usual disreputable-looking self. They also chose contrasting weapons: Ganryu had an excellent sword, while Musashi had only a rough wooden sword he had whittled into shape from a spare oar while sailing to the island.

Hundreds of curious onlookers turned out to watch the duel, but it was over in moments. Both men appeared to land blows at the same instant. However, only Ganryu fell, struck down by a powerful blow from Musashi's simple wooden sword. According to legend, Musashi turned away from his fallen rival and walked off without a word.

With this stunning victory, Musashi's first period of wandering came to an end. He traveled north to the temple city of Kyoto and settled, opening his own school of swordsmanship. In 1614, the swordsman resumed wandering, interspersed with short periods spent in service to various daimyo. While wandering, he fought still more duels and developed increasingly deep philosophical insights into his chosen profession. These meditations resulted in a book of wisdom and instruction, *Go Rin no Sho*, completed shortly before Musashi's death in 1645.

THE FORTY-SEVEN RONIN

Even if a samurai became just a ronin, that did not mean he necessarily lost his sense of loyalty to his master. A famous example concerns forty-seven samurai who avenged the murder of their lord. Their story (*Chushingura*, "vengeance") perfectly symbolizes the profound sacrifices and loyalty of the samurai spirit.

In 1701, two daimyo were ordered to arrange a reception in the shogun's castle in Edo. They were instructed in proper etiquette for the occasion by Yoshinaka Kira, an official in the Tokugawa shogunate. Kira became upset at the two, however, for reasons that are unclear. He was corrupt and may have been angry because they did not offer him money. In any event, instead of teaching them properly, he taunted and insulted them in public.

One daimyo, Asano, finally cracked under the abuse. Losing his temper, he attacked Kira with a dagger. He struck two blows before castle guards stopped him. Kira was only slightly wounded. Nonetheless, an attack on a high-ranking official within the shogun's castle was a grave offense and, despite a public outcry that he be treated with mercy, Asano was ordered to commit seppuku. After Asano died, his possessions were

The forty-seven ronin surround the home of Yoshinaka Kira to avenge their lord's murder. The samurai decapitated Kira after he refused to commit suicide.

confiscated and his family name was ruined. Some three hundred samurai under him became ronin. Forty-seven of these warriors vowed to avenge their lord by killing Kira.

Since Kira was suspicious, the ronin knew they would have to wait and catch him off-guard. Some found work as tradesmen or monks; others deliberately appeared to become harmless alcoholics. Spies reported these events back to Kira, who relaxed his guard. Then, in the guise of workmen and merchants, several ronin gained access to Kira's house and learned its layout. Others, meanwhile, secretly amassed weapons.

The band waited until December 1702 to launch their attack. Surrounding Kira's mansion during a driving snowstorm early one morning, they quickly overcame Kira's guards. Sixteen guards died and twenty-two were wounded. When the ronin searched the house, they found Kira hiding in a small storage building in a secret courtyard.

REVENGE

In consideration of Kira's rank, the leader of the ronin group offered to let the official honorably commit seppuku. The ronin leader even gave Kira the same dagger with which his late master, Asano, had killed himself. But Kira only crouched on the ground, speechless and trembling. His offer refused, the ronin leader then decapitated Kira. Taking Kira's head with them, the ronin headed to their lord's grave, in a temple elsewhere in the city. Word quickly spread, and on the way to the temple the ronin were showered with praise and offered refreshment by sympathetic citizens. At the temple, the ronin washed Kira's head and laid it on Asano's tomb. They offered

prayers and gave the temple's priest all their money, asking him to bury them decently. Then they turned themselves in to the authorities.

The forty-seven ronin had followed the ancient precepts of Bushido, remaining loyal to their master. On the other hand, they had specifically defied the shogun's authority by carefully planning a small war that, in his eyes, went beyond the boundaries of revenge carried out as a personal vendetta. Despite a number of petitions from admirers pleading for clemency, the samurai were sentenced to death. Early in 1703, the forty-seven ronin were allowed to commit seppuku. They were buried in front of the tomb of their master.

Stories about masterless samurai like the forty-seven ronin are colorful and instructive. However, the truth was that ronin were only a small minority of Japan's samurai class. The vast majority were regular soldiers with regular jobs—that is, preparing for and waging war.

CHAPTER 5

THE SAMURAI AT WAR

All samurai were expected to be ready for war at any time, even during the later centuries, when few full-scale battles were fought. Men who in peacetime served as bureaucrats, advisers, or even lowly servants had to be ready to pick up their weapons and travel to the field of battle at a moment's notice. This was what their whole lives pointed to, Stephen Turnbull notes: "[Warfare] was the situation for which the samurai had been trained since boyhood, the moment for which all the ancestral legends reserved their proudest language."[48]

CALLED UP

When a daimyo needed his troops, the announcement was typically made with war drums mounted in the tower of his castle. One *ashigaru* was assigned to beat out a signal for assembly. Since all samurai and their families were required to live in or near the castle grounds, there was no reason not to hear the summons.

Once assembled, the army formed into groups and began marching to the battleground. Generals—the highest-ranking warriors—and other mounted samurai went first, accompanied by attendants. Some of these attendants carried *nobori*, brightly colored banners bearing the daimyo's crest or family symbol.

Next came masses of archers and foot soldiers, as well as infantry armed with rifles, spears, and other weapons. Sometimes these infantrymen were peasants drafted on the spot. More typically, however, they were low-ranking samurai. Bringing up the rear were even lower-ranking samurai, such as cooks, messengers, and supply bearers.

The problems inherent in moving hundreds or thousands of soldiers together were daunting, and the daimyo and his generals faced constant difficulties. For example, existing roads in feudal Japan were usually crude paths at best. Roads frequently had to be improved or even created before a large army could move.

ALWAYS READY

The logistical problems of getting to the battlefield notwithstanding, a samurai was expected to be ready for combat at all times. In the early centuries of the samurai era, when most warriors lived on their own farms, it was said that they tilled rice in the fields with their spears stuck in the ground nearby and their sandals resting on top. In this way, they would be ready at a moment's notice to drop their farming implements and go to war.

Depending on his rank, a samurai was also expected to supply his daimyo with a certain number of weapons and lower-ranking men. It was his responsibility to scour the countryside for suitable men and supplies. By delegating this responsibility, the daimyo and the shogun above them could be assured of a large fighting force when needed without having to pay for a standing army.

The exact specifications changed over time, but they are typified by a schedule prepared in 1649 for the daimyo of the Tokugawa shogunate. The schedule gives the exact re-

A samurai prepares his page for battle. Samurai warriors were expected to supply lower-ranking men to serve as soldiers in the armies of their daimyo.

quirements expected of each rank. For instance, it states that a *hatamoto* (a member of the shogun's personal guard) was to be given an income of two thousand *koku.* In return, he was expected to be available for service at all times and was required to supply the following: eight samurai of *go-kenin* rank (*go-kenin* were personal servants); two armor bearers plus one reserve armor bearer; five spearmen plus one reserve spearman; four grooms; four baggage carriers; one sandal bearer; two *hasambiko* bearers plus one reserve bearer (a *hasambiko* was a traveling storage case); one archer; two soldiers armed with flintlocks; two bearers of ammunition; one *nodachi* (long sword) bearer; two *ashigaru* leaders; and one rain-hat carrier.

BAD FOOD AND UNCOMFORTABLE ARMOR

Feeding a large marching force was always a problem. Cooks for a samurai army could usually bring dried and salted fish along, and they might be able to negotiate with local farmers for produce. *Umeboshi* (pickled plums) were distributed whenever possible, because they were a good source of salt—an important consideration when marching or fighting in hot weather. If soldiers were very lucky, fresh deer or rabbit meat might be available. However, most field meals consisted of little more than rice, boiled or roasted over an open fire.

ᛉ ESCORTING A LORD ON THE ROAD ᛊ

A samurai serving his daimyo in wartime had many responsibilities. Some of his duties while en route to a battle were described by Yuzan Daidoji in his book Code of the Samurai:

When a samurai in service accompanies his lord on a journey and they arrive at a post-station it is most important that he should before sunset take care to make enquiries of the people of the locality, and note any hill or wood or shrine or temple and take his bearings by them, and find out in what direction from their lodging there is an open space and what is the condition of the road. This should be done so that should a fire suddenly break out during the night and it be necessary for his lord to retire he will be able to lead the way and know where to guide him.

And when he accompanies his lord on foot, to remember to go in front of him on a hill and behind him on a slope may seem a small matter, but it is one a retainer should not overlook. For it is the duty of a samurai to be vigilant and careful at all times to think out how he can render any possible service in the calling to which he is appointed.

While marching or awaiting battle, the samurai had other concerns besides food. For example, there was the difficulty of maintaining his armor. The silk cords that held the lamellae together were a constant worry. If they got wet, the cords were difficult to dry. They chafed uncomfortably in summer heat and felt freezing in the winter. Furthermore, they rotted easily and often housed lice and other bugs (which the samurai killed by smoking them out over a fire).

Other worries in the field included the possibility of disease, injury, or exhaustion. Soldiers were generally on their own when it came to questions of health, since doctors were available only to high-ranking warriors in the field. The lower ranks relied on folk remedies to treat injuries or illness. These remedies included eating horse dung, which was believed (erroneously) to stop bleeding, and bathing wounds in urine, which actually did cleanse the wound and inhibit the growth of bacteria.

BEFORE THE BATTLE

There was little opportunity to escape the hardships of a march. Even sleeping was a problem. While en route to a battle—a journey that could take weeks—a samurai usually slept on the ground with his helmet for a pillow. If they were lucky, higher-ranking soldiers might find a night's lodging in a temple or farmhouse. The highest-ranking generals sometimes stayed in guesthouses along the way or slept in tents that were carried with the rest of the supplies.

Once the army reached the battle site the higher-ranking warriors camped nearby in cloth tents. These tents offered only minimal protection from the elements. They were usually set up inside a circle of curtains and banners that bore the crest of the daimyo.

Despite their rough environment, elite warriors took great care with their personal appearance on the eve of a battle. Before facing the enemy, they always bathed carefully and often used perfume and makeup. Frequently, they also blackened their teeth—a mark of beauty in feudal Japan among both men and women.

A warrior had a very specific reason for this primping. If his head was taken in battle, the samurai wanted no reason for the enemy to mock his appearance. As Louis Fréderic writes, "It was fitting for a warrior to confront his enemy clean and perfumed."[49]

Another important prebattle ritual for a mounted samurai was to don his armor. A servant, typically a lower-ranking samurai, usually helped with this time-consuming task, which involved carefully putting on and securing the layers of clothing and individual pieces of armor. When danger was close, however, a samurai could leave most of his armor assembled on a rack, so that he could quickly put it on with minimal help.

INDIVIDUAL CHALLENGES

Generally, however, there was little chance that a samurai would have to rush into battle unprepared. When it came time for the battle, the opposing armies typically assembled on opposite sides of an agreed-upon plain. In earlier centuries, warriors observed certain very formal rules of engagement at such times. Typically, they began by assembling their armies (which were relatively small, compared to those in later centuries). Then each side fired a volley of special arrows that whistled loudly. This noise announced the formal opening of hostilities and carried the soldiers' prayers for good fortune to the gods.

Then individual warriors from both sides advanced on horseback to within a few hundred yards of each other and called out for worthy foes. In a typical encounter recorded by Louis Fréderic, a single horseman, beautifully dressed and armored, galloped near the enemy and announced: "Since I am a person of little consequence, it may be that not one among you knows my name. I am a vassal of the lord Ashikaga, Shidara Goro Saemon-no-Jo! If there is a vassal of the lords of Rokuhara among you who is willing to fight me, let him gallop forward without delay to test my skill!"

Hearing this challenge, a warrior on the opposing side came forward and cried out:

Although I am only an ignorant man, I have served for many years as Commissary of the Military Government. And although I am of inferior rank and may appear to be an insignificant foe in your eyes (for perhaps you despise me, thinking that I am only a lay-monk), I am descended from the family of General Toshihito, a family which, for many generations, has followed the Way of the Warrior. I belong to the seventeenth generation, I, Saito Genki, the lay-monk of Iyo! Why should I hold life dear in this battle which is to determine the fate of our two armies? If any are to be spared, let them all tell their sons and grandsons how honourably I fought.[50]

ON THE BATTLEFIELD

One after another, solo fights followed such challenges. Typically, two elite samurai charged each other on horseback. They shot arrows, though these usually inflicted only minor wounds on a well-armored man. If long-distance fighting was inconclusive, the samurai resorted to close combat by handing their bows to attendants and drawing their swords.

A seventeenth-century painting depicts samurai on the battlefield. Such large-scale battles became the norm in later samurai history.

More and more samurai would skirmish in this way, and soon a full-scale battle would be raging. Essentially, then, a battle was a collection of one-on-one duels, though there were many variations. For instance, several foot soldiers might attack a single mounted samurai. They would try to bring the samurai to the ground by cutting the legs of his horse with spears, or by using the rakelike *kumade*. Either way, the unhorsed samurai would be more vulnerable.

In later centuries, this style of battle changed dramatically. Strategy and weapons became more sophisticated,

❧ BURNING BRIDGES ❧

Sometimes, attacking armies went to great lengths to overcome a castle—and defending armies were just as intent on repelling the attackers. During the siege of Chihaya Castle in 1333, the attackers hired five hundred carpenters to build a suspension bridge. Five yards wide and sixty yards long, with two or three thousand ropes supporting it, the bridge spanned a deep valley that protected the castle.

However, the soldiers in the castle outwitted the attackers. They threw torches drenched in oil onto the bridge's girders. The bridge caught fire and fell into the valley, taking several thousand attacking soldiers with it. A contemporary account (quoted in Hiroaki Sato's *Legends of the Samurai*) asserted, "The spectacle was such that one could wonder if the Eight Great Hells were perhaps something like this—where criminals are said to be skewered on sword mountains and in saber trees, scorched in raging fires and cooked in molten iron baths."

and carefully planned conflicts between masses of troops—sometimes several thousand soldiers at a time—became the norm. Samurai historian Mitsuo Kure notes, "There were no more battle-opening ceremonies with shouted introductions and whistling arrows; there was no more drawing aside in battle for warriors to engage in personal duels."[51]

When advancing together, foot soldiers were especially vulnerable to attacks by bowmen and, in later centuries, soldiers armed with flintlocks. (The range of these weapons was about the same; both could be fired from a quarter-mile away with accuracy.) Foot soldiers had little protection except for their minimal armor and, sometimes, the large wooden shields they held out in front of themselves.

The highest-ranking samurai—the generals—usually took part in the fighting personally, but perhaps their most important role was to direct the action. Moving massive groups of soldiers quickly and effectively required careful planning and good communication techniques so that the generals could tell their troops what to do.

COMMUNICATION AND IDENTIFICATION

Generals and other leaders communicated with their troops in a variety of ways. Sometimes they used auditory signals, such as drums or trumpetlike blasts from conch shells. They also used visual signals, such as flags or large, ceremonial iron fans that could be seen from a distance.

Generals also needed to clearly identify, even from a great distance, which troops were theirs, so soldiers wore visible identification. For example, mounted samurai wore distinctive armor and helmets. Soldiers, especially those on foot, often wore tall, narrow banners called *sashimono* that bore the individual crest of their daimyo. These banners were mounted in bamboo frames on the soldiers' backs, so that their hands were free for battle.

A samurai wears armor specific to his position as a mounted soldier so he can be easily identified by his superiors.

Proper identification was not only important to the generals; it was crucial for all samurai. In the midst of a battle, they needed to know, quickly and decisively, who was who. In his manual for young samurai, the warrior-scholar Shigesuke Taira wrote, "In ancient codes for warrior houses it says that

This seventeenth-century screen illustrates that castles of the later years of samurai history were formidable, virtually impregnable structures.

those who are killed by their own allies because of neglecting recognition emblems have died for nothing."[52]

CASTLE WARFARE

Not all conflicts were pitched battles. The most effective way to capture a castle, for example, was with a siege. In a siege, attackers tried to starve castle occupants into submission by preventing supplies from going in (and, of course, by preventing those inside from leaving).

In the early centuries of the samurai era, sieges generally did not last long, because Japanese castles were little more than crude wooden fortresses and their defenses were easily overcome. However, in later centuries, samurai castles developed into complex, sophisticated, and sturdy structures. These buildings could withstand months of assault and often could store enough supplies to keep their occupants alive until the situation changed—perhaps when loyal reinforcements arrived from elsewhere.

Most samurai castles of the later years shared the same basic design: an elevated central complex surrounded by a maze of moats, walls, and gates that made attack difficult. They fell into one of two categories: mountain castles (*yamajiro*) or castles in plains or valleys (*hirajiro*). Typically, a bustling town, filled with artisans, merchants, and other peasants who served the daimyo and his samurai, surrounded the castle.

ATTACKING A CASTLE

Those attacking a castle had several powerful advantages. Perhaps the most important of these was the ability to replenish their troops, food, and supplies. The attacking samurai were rarely content simply to wait for castle occupants to starve or surrender, however; that was much too boring. Turnbull notes, "Carrying out a successful siege required a virtue found little in the samurai armory—patience. To sit down outside a wall and wait until one's opponent starved to death was a not particularly glorious undertaking."[53]

Not surprisingly, therefore, armies often went on the offensive. These direct assaults took many forms. Sometimes, samurai used catapults to hurl rocks or torches over the castle walls. On other occasions, they used tactics such as filling castle moats with bundles of rice grass so that the attackers could reach the castle walls.

Sometimes samurai leaders had to be creative while laying siege. One army commander had his troops divert a river so that it flooded out a castle. When the defending general surrendered, he sailed into the floodwaters below his castle and then killed himself in full view of the attackers.

DEFENDING A CASTLE

Samurai defending a castle, meanwhile, had certain advantages over their attackers. For example, from relative safety they could send arrows, rocks, or hot liquids down on those who tried to scale the walls. Stephen Turnbull relates one such encounter: "When the wall was about to fall, those within the castle took ladles with handles ten or twenty feet long, collected boiling water, and poured it on [the attackers]. The hot water passed through the holes in their helmet tops, ran down from the edges of their shoulder guards, and burned their bodies so severely that they fled in terror."[54]

On another occasion, according to Louis Fréderic, defending soldiers used their castle's own crumbling structure to their advantage: "In the end, the besiegers, filled with rage, grappled the wall on the four sides (of the fort) to scale it. But the men inside the fort cut all the ropes supporting the wall at the same time, for it was a double wall built in such a way as to let the outer one fall. . . . More than a thousand attackers were crushed under this weight."[55]

WINNING OR LOSING

Eventually, of course, battles or sieges ended with one side victorious. For the losers, the aftermath of a battle was grim. The site would be strewn with their dead and dying warriors and horses. Peasants often ran amid this bloody carnage, scavenging clothes and other useful items.

The victors, meanwhile, were jubilant. Often, there were celebrations and ceremonies to honor a particularly brave samurai. This warrior could expect a reward from his daimyo—perhaps a horse, sword, or banner.

However, the aftermath of a battle also involved cleanup work even for the victorious samurai. For one thing, they had to collect the severed heads of important enemies for display before their daimyo. Preparing these was an important and solemn ceremony typically performed by samurai women. They washed, combed, and applied makeup to the heads, then mounted each on a spiked wooden board and labeled it with the name of the fallen warrior.

On both the winning and losing sides, the names of the dead were recorded immediately after a battle. This was important because the authorities needed to compensate the soldiers' families; typically, each side compensated the families of its own fallen soldiers. This could be an enormous task; after five to six thousand soldiers were killed or wounded in a particular battle, one account relates, "when the war commissioner Nagasaki Shiro Saemon-no-Jo conducted his enquiry, twelve scribes were required to write down their names night and day for

A seventeenth-century painting depicts the siege of Osaka castle. The attackers have used flaming arrows to set fire to structures within the castle compound.

three days without putting down their brushes."[56]

DESERTION OR DEATH

In most cases, the number of wounded to be recorded—at least on the losing side—was small. Most wounded soldiers did not survive. They were often killed outright by the victors, usually by decapitation, although sometimes—despite the strictures of Bushido—victorious armies preferred to torture their prisoners first. Common tortures included forcing prisoners to walk on hot coals and crucifying them head downward.

❧ AN UNCHANGING PRINCIPLE ☙

A samurai always tried to maintain strict principles of loyalty and courage, even in the most difficult wartime circumstances. These principles are illustrated by a letter written by Torii Mototada to his son while defending Fushimi Castle in 1600. It is quoted in Stephen Turnbull's The Lone Samurai and the Martial Arts:

I am resolved to make a stand inside the castle, and to die. . . . It would not be difficult to break through the enemy and escape. . . . But that is not the true meaning of being a warrior. Instead I shall hold out against the strength of the whole country, without even one hundredth part of the men who would be needed to do so, and I shall defend it and die a glorious death. . . . Thus I will have taken an initiative that will strengthen the resolve of Ieyasu's other retainers. . . . It is not the Way of the Warrior to be shamed and avoid death. . . . To sacrifice one's life for one's master is an unchanging principle.

Sometimes, unwounded soldiers from the losing side were taken prisoner. On rare occasions, a captured samurai defied the normal laws of Bushido. Along with the men under him, he would join the winning side. One such instance involved a victory on the part of the samurai Kusunoki: "[Kusunoki's enemy] the lay-monk of Yuasa, now beset on all sides by his enemies, yielded his neck (meaning removed his helmet) as a sign of surrender. After Kusunoki had taken over this monk's warriors with his 700 horsemen, he brought into subjection the two provinces of Izumi and Kawachi and his army became exceedingly strong."[57]

A LAST POEM

Joining the enemy, however, was unusual. Even if, in keeping with the gentle precepts of Bushido, a captive was not tortured, he still faced dishonor if he was taken alive. To avert this, those facing defeat typically tried to commit suicide first, perhaps by throwing themselves off a cliff or by deliberately falling on their swords from their horses. H. Paul Varley writes, "[Samurai] held few things in greater contempt than capture or surrender, and it came to be universally expected of warriors that they be prepared to destroy themselves to avoid falling into enemy hands."[58]

For high-ranking samurai, the choice was a little better. They were usually allowed to commit seppuku—always a better death than mere execution. Often, the condemned warrior was allowed to write a last poem. One example was a famous samurai named Tomoyuki. Preparing for death, Tomoyuki composed farewell verses that reflected Buddhist teachings:

> For forty-two years I have dwelt
>
> In this mortal sphere of non-action.
>
> Heaven and earth pass away

When I say my farewell to life.[59]

For several centuries, the samurai was a true warrior, a soldier whose primary job was fighting. However, that job changed in the early 1600s, after the Tokugawa shogunate created a lasting, nationwide peace. With the need for battle virtually gone, the samurai still stood ready to fight, but their primary role was as a class of bureaucrats—powerful, proud, and sometimes violent, but bureaucrats nonetheless.

CHAPTER 6

THE SAMURAI AS BUREAUCRAT

With the fall of Osaka Castle in 1615, the shogun Ieyasu eliminated his last potential rivals for power; essentially all of Japan's daimyo came under his control. Following that decisive victory, there were no major upheavals of Japan's social order for some 250 years. The Tokugawa era was a time of relative peace for the nation, as Ieyasu and his successors maintained strict military control.

Since there was little conflict, the samurai of the Tokugawa era were almost never called on to apply their skills as warriors. Instead, their peacetime positions evolved into permanent positions as the samurai took on a variety of new, full-time roles. Nonetheless, the samurai of the Tokugawa era were still expected to be ready at any moment to resume active duty. This was partly because the authorities were constantly fearful that Japan might return to civil war and chaos. The shoguns lived in constant fear that rebellious daimyo, or discontented peasants or ronin, might stage an uprising.

The shoguns therefore created a number of deterrents meant to squelch uprisings before they began. One of these deterrents was the existence of a permanent reserve army. Writer Clive Sinclaire notes, "Every samurai was expected to be ready for mortal combat on behalf of his lord at a moment's notice, even if his [peacetime] position within the clan was only that of a clerk. They were encouraged to think of themselves as 'already dead,' so that they had nothing to lose in combat, which offered them the opportunity of a glorious death in the service of their lord."[60]

NEW JOBS

As the shogunate settled into its long peacetime reign, the majority of samurai became full-time government employees. They served as bureaucrats, diplomats, officials, and other court attendants. These positions were almost always hereditary; a samurai's specific job was typically similar to the one his father and grandfather had held when they were not at war.

Under this new system, a typical samurai's day was largely spent in dull, mundane pursuits. These were the equivalent of today's desk jobs: tabulating data, attending formal functions, and carrying out other routine duties. Louis Fréderic describes a few typical positions: "The samurai . . . spent their time managing the administrative, legal and economic affairs of their domains and household.

Deprived of their livelihood as soldiers during the peaceful years of the Tokugawa era, many samurai like these took on government jobs.

They received the tax or revenue from their lands in kind (rice, silk, hemp, fabric, land or sea produce), sometimes in money."[61] Other typical jobs involved more physical activity, such as performing guard duty, collecting taxes, conducting training, and patrolling outlying frontier regions.

Once, the samurai had been experts at warfare. Over time, however, the old military ways became little more than legends. The samurai turned their attention increasingly to becoming experts at diplomacy, intrigue, and politics. For a young samurai, training in politics, the arts, and education thus became as important—or more so—as battle skills. Yuzan Daidoji wrote,

When the land is at war he must be in the camp and the field day and night and can never know a moment's rest. . . . All ranks have to work continuously as fast and as strenuously as possible. But in peaceful times there is no camp duty and consequently . . . the various ranks under their commanders are allotted to fixed duties as guards, escorts, inspectors, and the like, and come to regard these stay-at-home functions as the normal ones for a warrior family, and think of field service as nothing but a dream of the past.[62]

SOMETIMES IN THE CAPITAL, SOMETIMES AT HOME

One of the regular functions of the samurai who served as bureaucrats was appearing at ceremonial functions, decked out in full armor. It was one of the few times a warrior still had a chance to wear a full suit of armor. Typical of such ceremonies were the formal processions that the daimyo mounted to show themselves to the people. The most common of these processions were regular, enforced pilgrimages between the capital of Edo (known today as Tokyo) and the daimyo's individual country estates.

These regular processions to and from the capital were required as part of a Tokugawa system called *sankin kotai*, meaning roughly "serving the lord in shifts." According to this system, the wives and children of all of Japan's daimyo were required to live in the capital. However, the daimyo were not allowed to live with their families full-time.

Each daimyo was required instead to live part-time in Edo and part-time in his own native region. The exact periods of stay in each place differed, depending on how far an individual daimyo's home was from the capital. (Another factor was how deeply in or out of favor the daimyo was with the shogun.)

Some daimyo were required to spend one full year in Edo, then the next year at home. Sometimes, a daimyo whose home was near Edo was required to spend only six months in the capital and six months at home. Meanwhile, those daimyo whose land was very distant had more relaxed rules. For example, a daimyo from faraway Kyushu might be required to spend only four months out of every three years in Edo.

CONTROLLING THE DAIMYO

The *sankin kotai* arrangement was part of a complex system that allowed the shoguns to assert control over the daimyo. The shoguns were always careful to ensure that their daimyo could not become too powerful or entertain thoughts of rebellion.

The alternate attendance arrangement helped ensure that the odds of a serious rebellion were low in several ways. For one thing, no daimyo was likely to get ideas about overthrowing the shogunate if his family was kept as a virtual hostage in the capital city. Also, *sankin-kotai* was a very expensive arrangement for the daimyo. Most daimyo were forced to spend a great deal of time and money on travel to and fro—time and money that could not be spent in plotting a rebellion.

PART OF THE JOB

For the samurai who served under a given daimyo, these time-consuming processions—which involved large

❧ "RUBBING ❧ THE BACKS OF THE HANDS"

A warrior's duty during the early period of the samurai era—primarily fighting—was very different from the bureaucratic duty of a samurai during the later Tokugawa era. The samurai Yuzan Daidoji pointed this out in his book Code of the Samurai:

Now the samurai of the civil war period were in the field innumerable times in their day and risked their lives freely for their lords and commanders but they did not talk about their merit or their valiant deeds. And peacetime service is merely shuffling about on the mats, rubbing the backs of the hands, and fighting battles with three inches of tongue for better or worse, and certainly nothing like risking one's life in war. But whether in peace or war it is the duty of the samurai to serve in just the same spirit of loyalty.

retinues of soldiers and servants—were simply a regular part of the job. It was up to high-ranking samurai leaders to organize these massive undertakings, and the samurai under them were required to conduct them

with as much pomp and ceremony as possible.

Yuzan Daidoji, in his handbook for young samurai, noted his opinion that the expense of such a procession should be borne by all the samurai under a daimyo. Reflecting the traditional creed of Bushido, he wrote,

In times of peace a military procession makes a brave show and people from the country come crowding into the houses of the town to see it, so that it is exposed to the view of all classes, and if our array is inferior to the others it is a lifelong shame to the lord and his captains.

Under the system of sankin kotai, *each daimyo was required to spend part of the year in Edo (pictured), the capital of feudal Japan.*

every possible hardship, for it is the duty of all who are in the service of a lord to bend all their energies to keep his affairs in proper order.[63]

So when we consider all this and its importance, all samurai, both great and small, old retainers and recently joined ones, must not fail to contribute a suitable proportion of their salary. And during this period of reduced income everyone has to use his brains a little and . . . put up with

RELICS OF A FORMER TIME

Even though they were no longer full-time soldiers, the samurai were still allowed the trappings of a warrior elite. For instance, they could wear at all times the two swords that symbolized their social position. (The samurai were still the only class whose members were allowed to carry or own swords.) The samurai were also allowed to retain official titles that made them sound as though they were still real warriors. For example, a senior administrative official in the finance department of a daimyo might have the grandiose title of *uma-mawari*—"horse-mounted guard"—even though he was, in reality, little more than a deskbound functionary.

The titles were little more than window dressing, however. Despite such honorific trappings, the samurai faced an uphill battle in maintaining their elite positions within Japanese society. By the early eighteenth century, the country was changing, thanks to a rapidly growing merchant economy. Amid a new, booming, vibrant urban culture, a wealthy merchant class, once nearly the lowest stratum of society, was rising rapidly in status. In light of these changes, the austere lifestyle of the samurai was increasingly considered by many to be quaint and old-fashioned. The samurai were still prominent, honored members of society. However, they were increasingly seen as irrelevant relics of a former time who were rapidly losing their long-enjoyed status and power.

MOONLIGHTING

At the same time, the samurai were suffering financially. For centuries, they had depended on their stipends—the fixed amounts of goods or money provided to them by their daimyo. However, the stipend system for the samurai began to erode as their importance in society diminished.

Under the stipend system, samurai had been expected to maintain certain standards of living. These standards were dictated by the daimyo in great detail, even down to the number of horses and servants a samurai household was expected to maintain. As times changed, high-ranking samurai could maintain these standards fairly easily. However, this was not true for the lower ranks of the samurai. They grew increasingly impoverished. Some were so poor that they were even forced to pawn their swords.

Nearly all of these lower-ranking samurai were, at one time or another, forced to moonlight with second or even third jobs to make ends meet. Some made such items as toys, lanterns, or umbrellas. Others learned carpentry, sandal making, or other trades. Still others found work as gatekeepers or private bodyguards. And a smaller number became teachers, poets, scholars, monks, physicians, or artists.

Although martial arts were no longer necessary battle skills, studying the martial arts was still considered an excellent way to instill character and discipline in young people. As a result, a number of samurai opened schools devoted to one or another of the martial arts. An eighteenth-century poet captured the flavor of the changing times for martial artists when he wrote:

Sweat dripping down

As you drill away at the arts of the sword;

That they're no use,

May this reign be praised.[64]

"THEIR FEARFUL APPEARANCE AND THRUST-OUT ELBOWS"

A relatively small number of samurai did not settle into jobs within the bureaucracy, or find legitimate work, or become entrepreneurs on their own. Some became ronin, rootless freelancers, while others took to petty crime and became little more than gangsters. The samurai Sorai Ogyu denounced the bad behavior he noticed among some of these men, writing: "They conduct themselves in the town with their fearful appearance and thrust-out elbows. With their power to punish they suppress people and create disorder in society."[65]

Increasing poverty and the difficulty of adjusting to the reality of a wealthy, prestigious middle class also took their toll on the code of the samurai. It became increasingly difficult for the warriors of old to adhere

๑ EASIER ๖ TIMES

In this passage from his book Code of the Samurai, *the samurai and scholar Yuzan Daidoji comments on how much easier samurai life was in his day compared to earlier times. This easier life did not, in his opinion, excuse his fellow samurai from maintaining their tradition of hard work and diligence:*

The warriors who were born [before the Tokugawa era] were always in the field, scorched in their armor under the summer skies or pierced through its chinks by the winter blasts, soaked by the rain and cloaked by the snow, sleeping on moor and hill with no pillow but their mailed sleeve and with nothing to eat or drink but unhulled rice and salt soup. And whether they had to fight in the field or to attack a fortress or defend one they thought it no special hardship or trial but all in the ordinary day's work.

When we reflect on this and how we, born in times of peace, can sleep under a mosquito net in summer and wrap ourselves in quilts in winter, and in fact live at ease eating what we fancy at any time of day, we should indeed consider ourselves lucky. But there is no reason why we should regard indoor guard duty or inspecting in the neighborhood as a serious burden.

to the ideals of Bushido, especially since there was little use for their traditional martial skills.

Within decades of the beginning of the Tokugawa era, therefore, samurai began to notice a decline in the standards of their class. Regular practice in martial arts dropped so dramatically that in 1694 a law actually was passed that required the samurai to practice these skills. One warrior, Tsunetomo Yamamoto, complained in 1716, "Now when young samurai get together, if there is not just talk about money matters, loss and gain, secrets, clothing styles or matters of sex, there is no reason to gather together at all. Customs are going to pieces."[66] Another samurai, Seifu Murata, lamented of his colleagues that "only the swords in their belts reminded them that they were samurai."[67]

A number of solutions were proposed to reverse this downward slide. Banzan Kumazawa, a seventeenth-century warrior who served the Ikeda family, advocated letting the samurai go back to being part-time farmers. He wrote, "Even since the samurai and the farmers have become separate classes, the samurai have become sickly and their hands and feet have grown weak."[68]

WESTERN INFLUENCES

Despite efforts to change the trend, however, the shifts in Japanese society were too strong to be effectively resisted. In the eyes of many observers, these shifts were accelerated when, beginning in the mid-1700s, Japan slowly began opening its ports to foreigners and allowing Western influences to enter. This gradual opening came after long centuries of isolation, when the country had been almost completely cut off from new technology or ways of thinking.

Without a doubt, the changes in Japanese society caused by Western influences had a dramatic impact on the warrior class. Stephen Turnbull comments, "The last century of Tokugawa rule was a time of crisis for the samurai."[69] Indeed, the increasing influence of Western culture in Japan closely paralleled the end of the samurai era.

Many people in Japan—those in positions of authority and others—passionately objected to the opening of the country's ports to foreigners. They wanted Japan to remain a closed and, in their eyes, pure society. A number of countries, including Russia, tried to open relations with Japan; the point was forced, finally, in 1853.

That year, an officer in the U.S. Navy, Commodore Matthew Perry, sailed a small fleet of ships into Tokyo Bay. He delivered a firm message to the shogun: America was eager to start a trade and diplomatic relationship with Japan. The Tokugawa government, unsure how to proceed with the foreigners, failed to reach a quick decision about Perry's demands. The shogunate came under intense pressure from a variety of sources, including a Japanese middle class eager to take advantage of trade and technological innovations from the West.

Under such pressure, the last Tokugawa shogun was forced to resign in 1868. Following this momentous development, political power was quickly restored to the reigning emperor, Meiji. He was able to bring the nation back under his control and welcome trade with Western nations. Thus Western influences, directly and indirectly, brought an end to the shogunate, to Japan's feudal system, and, eventually, to the samurai.

THE MEIJI RESTORATION

Following the resignation of the shogun, massive changes to society—

Commodore Matthew Perry's fleet sails into Tokyo Bay in 1853. Perry's arrival signaled the demise of Japanese feudal society.

❧ THE FIVE ARTICLES OATH ❧

In April 1868, the newly powerful Emperor Meiji issued a proclamation that was the virtual death sentence for the samurai as a separate, privileged class. The so-called Five Articles Oath of 1868 is reproduced in "Origins and Significance of the Meiji Restoration," an article by Colin Barker at www.marxists.de/fareast/barker/pt4.htm:

Deliberative assemblies shall be widely established and all matters decided by public discussion.

All classes, high and low, shall unite in vigorously carrying out the administration of affairs of state.

The common people, no less than the civil and military officials, shall each be allowed to pursue his own calling so that there may be no discontent.

Evil customs of the past shall be broken off and everything based upon the just laws of nature.

Knowledge shall be sought throughout the world so as to strengthen the foundations of imperial rule.

In 1868 Emperor Meiji formally abolished the samurai class.

a movement known to historians as the Meiji Restoration—resulted in swift changes to the samurai class. Any semblance of their old military power disappeared, and in 1868 the emperor formally abolished the samurai class. In its place, he created a modernized, Western-style army. This new force was made up of soldiers chosen from all over the country and from all classes. Trained by Western military experts, the new army was adept at using guns and other modern weapons.

When the samurai were formally abolished, they were forced to give up their distinctive hairstyles, in which their foreheads were shaved and the hair on the sides worn long. The warriors also lost their yearly stipends. Perhaps most humiliating of all, they were no longer allowed to carry swords, their ancient symbol of power; members of the new army were to be the only armed people in Japan. The feudal system as a whole came under attack and was dismantled; it was officially abolished in 1871.

Naturally, the samurai did not take these changes lightly. They had long felt that the influence of the West was dangerous to their well-established social order. For years before the end of the shogunate, therefore, the samurai had been vocal about what they saw as corrupting, invasive influences. Summarizing the situation, writer Harry Cook notes that the samurai

"were an integral part of a feudal system that depended upon a strict separation of classes and the concentration of military technology and power in the hands of a few. An open country, actively seeking knowledge from abroad, would be susceptible to rapid change, and change would destroy the raison d' être [reason for existence] of the samurai."[70]

A LAST STAND

Despite their objections, the samurai were virtually powerless to prevent the massive changes happening in Japanese society. Many simply chose to go along with the new order as best they could. They blended in with the new regime, taking on influential positions in the new army and government. Others, however, resisted change as long as possible. This old guard, which hoped to return Japan to the days of the samurai, made several last attempts at restoring the old order. The most significant of these was the Satsuma rebellion of 1877.

This uprising pitted a group of rebellious samurai from the southern regions of Japan (including the province of Satsuma) against the newly formed, Western-style army and several prominent daimyo. It required seven months of intense fighting and heavy losses on both sides before the imperial army, supplied as it was with firearms, finally defeated the rebels. Finally forced to admit defeat, the

rebel leader committed seppuku on the battlefield. He and his comrades had put up a noble fight, but in the end they were no match for the emperor's army. Clive Sinclaire comments, "The samurai and their swords were simply out of date and out of step with modern warfare."[71]

THE SPIRIT CONTINUES

Despite the rapid changes and the decline in importance of the samurai, the influence of this fierce warrior class remained strong in Japan. More than sixty years after the final rebellion at Satsuma, the samurai spirit was still evident in the modified form of Bushido Japanese soldiers maintained in World War II. Many soldiers in that conflict emulated the samurai by volunteering for suicide missions, willingly surrendering their lives in the service of their country. Clive Sinclaire comments, "During

Satsuma rebels surrender to the emperor's army in 1877. The swords of the samurai rebels were no match for the modern weaponry of the emperor's army.

the Pacific War, every Japanese soldier had his chance to be a samurai warrior, however briefly."[72]

The importance and influence of the samurai spirit continue to this day. Japan scholar Thomas Cleary asserts, "Even today the conventional Japanese culture and mentality cannot be understood without recognizing the residual influence of those samurai centuries."[73] Some warrior bloodlines, such as the Honda family, still have significant influence in Japanese business, society, and politics. In some rural areas of the country, the descendants of samurai families are still treated with a special form of respect reminiscent of the glory days of the Tokugawa shogunate. And in novels, movies, and stories, the ancient samurai are still honored as great warriors and legendary keepers of the Bushido spirit.

NOTES

INTRODUCTION: THE RISE OF THE SAMURAI CLASS

1. Louis Fréderic, *Daily Life in Japan at the Time of the Samurai.* New York: Praeger, 1972, p. 21.
2. Quoted in Stephen Turnbull, *The Book of the Samurai: The Warrior Class of Japan.* New York: Gallery Books, 1982, p. 47.
3. H. Paul Varley, *Samurai.* New York: Delacorte, 1970, p. 22.
4. Turnbull, *The Book of the Samurai,* p. 89.
5. Turnbull, *The Book of the Samurai,* p. 8.

CHAPTER 1: TRAINING FOR WAR

6. Varley, *Samurai,* p. 43.
7. Oscar Ratti and Adele Westbrook, *Secrets of the Samurai.* Rutland, VT: Tuttle, 1973, p. 15.
8. Quoted in Varley, *Samurai,* p. 105.
9. Quoted in Clive Sinclaire, *Samurai: The Weapons and Spirit of the Japanese Warrior.* Guilford, CT: Lyons Press, 2001, p. 40.
10. Harry Cook, *Samurai: The Story of a Warrior Tradition.* New York: Sterling, 1993, p. 32.
11. Inazo Nitobe, *Bushido: The Soul of Japan.* Rutland, VT: Tuttle, 1969, p. 32.

12. Shigesuke Taira, *Code of the Samurai: A Modern Translation of the Bushido Shoshinshu of Taira Shigesuke,* trans. Thomas Cleary. Boston: Tuttle, 1999, p. 95.
13. Quoted in "Samurai House Codes (kakun)," www.columbia.edu/~hds2/chushinguranew/Bushido/Kakun.htm.
14. Fréderic, *Daily Life in Japan at the Time of the Samurai,* p. 37.
15. Quoted in "Samurai House Codes (kakun)."
16. Yuzan Daidoji, *Code of the Samurai,* trans. A.L. Sadler. Rutland, VT: Tuttle, 1988, pp. 22–23.
17. Cook, *Samurai,* p. 6.

CHAPTER 2: BUSHIDO: THE WAY OF THE WARRIOR

18. Mitsuo Kure, *Samurai: An Illustrated History.* Boston: Tuttle, 2001, p. 10.
19. Daidoji, *Code of the Samurai,* p. 105.
20. Quoted in Stephen Turnbull, *The Lone Samurai and the Martial Arts.* London: Arms and Armour Press, 1990, p. 106.
21. Nitobe, *Bushido,* p. 5.
22. Taira, *Code of the Samurai,* p. 22.
23. Quoted in Nitobe, *Bushido,* pp. 36–37.

24. Cook, *Samurai*, p. 134.
25. Quoted in Nitobe, *Bushido*, p. 30.
26. Fréderic, *Daily Life in Japan at the Time of the Samurai*, p. 195.
27. Quoted in Hiroaki Sato, *Legends of the Samurai*. Woodstock, NY: Overlook Press, 1995, p. xxiii.
28. Quoted in "Samurai House Codes (kakun)."
29. Quoted in Cook, *Samurai*, p. 38.
30. Taira, *Code of the Samurai*, p. 60.
31. *Taira, Code of the Samurai*, pp. 10–11.
32. Fréderic, *Daily Life in Japan at the Time of the Samurai*, pp. 162–163.
33. Varley, *Samurai*, p. 24.
34. Sinclaire, *Samurai*, p. 14.
35. Fréderic, *Daily Life in Japan at the Time of the Samurai*, pp. 163–64.
36. Quoted in "Samurai House Codes (kakun)."

CHAPTER 3:
SAMURAI RANKS AND WEAPONS
37. Fréderic, *Daily Life in Japan at the Time of the Samurai*, p. 159.
38. Daidoji, *Code of the Samurai*, p. 53.
39. Turnbull, *The Book of the Samurai*, p. 19.
40. Kure, *Samurai*, p. 86.
41. Daidoji, *Code of the Samurai*, p. 39.
42. Quoted in Cook, *Samurai*, p. 72.
43. Sinclaire, *Samurai*, p. 42.
44. Quoted in Turnbull, *The Book of the Samurai*, p. 66.
45. Turnbull, *The Lone Samurai and the Martial Arts*, p. 98.

CHAPTER 4: THE RONIN
46. Turnbull, *The Lone Samurai and the Martial Arts*, pp. 61–62.
47. Turnbull, *The Lone Samurai and the Martial Arts*, p. 70.

CHAPTER 5:
THE SAMURAI AT WAR
48. Turnbull, *The Lone Samurai and the Martial Arts*, p. 6.
49. Fréderic, *Daily Life in Japan at the Time of the Samurai*, p. 56.
50. Quoted in Fréderic, *Daily Life in Japan at the Time of the Samurai*, pp. 182–83.
51. Kure, *Samurai*, p. 75.
52. Taira, *Code of the Samurai*, pp. 42–43.
53. Turnbull, *The Book of the Samurai*, p. 67.
54. Quoted in Turnbull, *The Lone Samurai and the Martial Arts*, pp. 34–36.
55. Fréderic, *Daily Life in Japan at the Time of the Samurai*, p. 187.
56. Quoted in Fréderic, *Daily Life in Japan at the Time of the Samurai*, p. 190.
57. Quoted in Fréderic, *Daily Life in Japan at the Time of the Samurai*, p. 189.
58. Varley, *Samurai*, p. 33.
59. Quoted in Fréderic, *Daily Life in Japan at the Time of the Samurai*, p. 192.

CHAPTER 6:
THE SAMURAI AS BUREAUCRAT
60. Sinclaire, *Samurai*, p. 20.

61. Fréderic, *Daily Life in Japan at the Time of the Samurai*, p. 60.
62. Daidoji, *Code of the Samurai*, pp. 82–83.
63. Daidoji, *Code of the Samurai*, p. 78.
64. Quoted in Cook, *Samurai*, p. 111.
65. Quoted in Turnbull, *The Lone Samurai and the Martial Arts*, p. 91.
66. Quoted in Cook, *Samurai*, p. 115.
67. Quoted in Turnbull, *The Lone Samurai and the Martial Arts*, p. 91.
68. Quoted in Turnbull, *The Lone Samurai and the Martial Arts*, pp. 108–109.
69. Turnbull, *The Book of the Samurai*, p. 150.
70. Cook, *Samurai*, p. 122.
71. Sinclaire, *Samurai*, p. 58.
72. Sinclaire, *Samurai*, p. 25.
73. Thomas Cleary, "Introduction," in Taira, *Code of the Samurai*, p. xv.

FOR FURTHER READING

BOOKS

Eleanor J. Hall, *Life Among the Samurai.* San Diego: Lucent Books, 1997. An entertaining and clearly written book in Lucent's The Way People Live series.

Andrew Haslam and Clare Doran, *Make It Work: Old Japan.* New York: Thomson Learning, 1995. An interesting book of projects to make clothes, models of boats, musical instruments, and other items associated with samurai-era Japan.

Erik Haugaard, *The Revenge of the Forty-seven Samurai.* Boston: Houghton Mifflin, 1995. A lively retelling, from the point of view of a young boy, of the famous story about a group of ronin who plot a bloody revenge for their master's death.

———, *The Samurai's Tale.* Boston: Houghton Mifflin, 1984. This novel for young adults concerns a young samurai in sixteenth-century Japan who loses his status when his family is killed.

Fiona McDonald, John James, and David Antram, *Inside Story: A Samurai Castle.* New York: Peter Bedrick Books, 1995. A nicely illustrated look in detail at the making and workings of a samurai-era castle.

WEB SITES

Electric Samurai (www.kiku.com/ electric_samurai/index.html). A site maintained by samurai buffs in Japan, with dozens of entries including photos of samurai-related shrines and paintings of famous samurai (complete with charmingly cracked English captions).

Kyoto National Museum (www.kyo haku.go.jp). This site (which can be viewed with English text) has wonderful photos of priceless Japanese treasures, including many items from the samurai era.

WORKS CONSULTED

BOOKS

Harry Cook, *Samurai: The Story of a Warrior Tradition.* New York: Sterling, 1993. A well-illustrated, episodic history by a journalist and martial arts expert.

Yuzan Daidoji, *Code of the Samurai.* Trans. A.L. Sadler. Rutland, VT: Tuttle, 1988. A modern translation of an early eighteenth-century text for young warriors.

Louis Fréderic, *Daily Life in Japan at the Time of the Samurai.* New York: Praeger, 1972. An English translation of a classic work by a French historian.

Mitsuo Kure, *Samurai: An Illustrated History.* Boston: Tuttle, 2001. This excellent, detailed introduction to the subject has lavish illustrations, including photographs of men in reproduction samurai armor from various periods.

Dave Lowry, *Autumn Lightning: The Education of an American Samurai.* Boston: Shambhala, 2001. This memoir of a modern-day American's study of Japanese martial arts includes many stories about renowned samurai.

Inazo Nitobe, *Bushido: The Soul of Japan.* Rutland, VT: Tuttle, 1969. A book-length meditation on Bushido by a Japanese scholar, first published in 1905, with many references to Western philosophy and literature.

Oscar Ratti and Adele Westbrook, *Secrets of the Samurai.* Rutland, VT: Tuttle, 1973. This is an extremely detailed and scholarly look at the martial arts of feudal Japan.

Hiroaki Sato, *Legends of the Samurai.* Woodstock, NY: Overlook Press, 1995. A fascinating compendium of writings from the samurai era, translated and annotated by a distinguished translator of Japanese poetry.

Clive Sinclaire, *Samurai: The Weapons and Spirit of the Japanese Warrior.* Guilford, CT: Lyons Press, 2001. This heavily illustrated book focuses on weaponry.

Shigesuke Taira, *Code of the Samurai: A Modern Translation of the Bushido Shoshinshu of Taira Shigesuke.* Trans. Thomas Cleary. Boston: Tuttle, 1999. This handbook, whose title translates as "Bushido for Beginners," was written in the early eighteenth century.

Stephen Turnbull, *The Book of the Samurai: The Warrior Class of Japan.*

New York: Gallery Books, 1982. A thorough, clearly written, informative, and well-illustrated book by a noted expert.

————, *The Lone Samurai and the Martial Arts.* London: Arms and Armour Press, 1990. This is a fairly specialized book that focuses on the concept of the samurai as a lone wolf.

————, *Samurai Warriors.* London: Blandford Press, 1987. The full-color illustrations in this book illuminate the costumes of many ranks of the samurai class throughout the centuries. The text focuses on the histories of individual outstanding samurai.

H. Paul Varley, *Samurai.* New York: Delacorte, 1970. A good, concise introduction by a distinguished historian.

WEB SITES

Bushido Home Page (http://mcel.pacificu.edu/as/students/bushido/bindex.html). Part of a site maintained by the Asian studies department of Pacific University in Oregon.

Origins and Significance of the Meiji Restoration (www.marxists.de/fareast/barker/pt4.htm). This article by Colin Barker is part of a Web site resource for political science scholars.

Samurai Archives Japanese History Page (www.samurai-archives.com). An extremely detailed and scholarly site, covering many topics such as famous samurai, family crests, weapons, genealogy, and martial arts.

Samurai House Codes (www.columbia.edu/~hds2/chushinguranew/Bushido/Kakun.htm). This is part of a Web site maintained by Dr. Henry Smith of Columbia University.

INDEX

ABOUT THE AUTHOR

Adam Woog has written more than forty books for adults, teens, and children. For Lucent Books, he has explored subjects including Louis Armstrong, Prohibition, Anne Frank, Elvis Presley, sweatshops, and the New Deal.

Woog lived in Japan for many years and now lives with his family in Seattle, Washington, his hometown.